Jim —

Glad you could join us!

DM

Thanks for being part of our event.

David K

Thanks!
Lesley

Thanks so much!
Kristina

Thanks very much!
Sara

Glad we could have you with us!
Darren

Thank you!
Kristin

We are excited to have you at our event!
Nicholas

NEW MEXICO
a guide for the eyes™

New Mexico:
A Guide for the Eyes

Second Edition
©2011 Elisa Parhad

Printed in China

ISBN: 978-0-9820497-1-6
Library of Congress Control Number: 2008940768

Published by EyeMuse Books
1630 Cicero Drive
Los Angeles, CA 90026
www.eyemusebooks.com

22101140

NEW MEXICO

a guide for the eyes™

Elisa Parhad

eyemuse books

Los Angeles, California

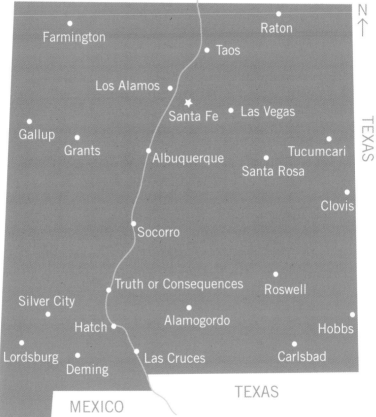

COLORADO

N

Raton

Farmington

Taos

Los Alamos

Santa Fe

Las Vegas

Gallup

Grants

Albuquerque

Tucumcari

Santa Rosa

Clovis

ARIZONA

TEXAS

Socorro

Truth or Consequences

Roswell

Silver City

Alamogordo

Hatch

Hobbs

Lordsburg

Deming

Las Cruces

Carlsbad

MEXICO

TEXAS

TO JORDAN, WHO BELIEVED IN ME.

TABLE OF CONTENTS

STRUCTURES

1 Acequia
3 Adobe
7 Arroyo
17 Blue Doors
37 Cliff Dwelling
51 Coyote Fence
57 Earthship
65 Hogan
69 Horno
75 Indian Casino
83 Kiva
85 Kiva Fireplace
101 Mission Church
103 Morada
111 Nicho
117 Pawnshop
131 Pueblo
133 Pueblo Ladder
137 Pueblo Revival Style
139 Queen Anne Style
141 Railroad
145 Ranch Gate
153 Route 66
175 Talavera Tile
179 Territorial Style
181 Tin Roofs
189 Viga

TRADITIONS

35 Classic Pickup
   Truck
53 Curanderismo
71 Hot Air Balloon
93 Lowrider
95 Luminaria
99 Milagro
113 Nuclear Science
121 Petroglyph
143 Rain Cloud Motif
147 Ristra
151 Roadside Memorial
157 Sand Painting
165 Smudge Stick
195 Zia Symbol

WEARABLES

21 Bolo Tie
39 Concho
41 Corn Necklace
43 Cowboy Boots
45 Cowboy Buckle
47 Cowboy Hat
119 Pendleton Blanket
161 Silver Jewelry
169 Squash Blossom
    Necklace

PREFACE

In 2001 I was living in rural Japan, working as an English teacher. Soon after my arrival, I began to notice unfamiliar imagery that reached far beyond my knowledge of the country's better-known icons. Among the many things I saw that caused me to pause and ask, "What is this? What does this mean?" was the statue of a Buddha dressed in a red hat and a bib.

The first time I saw the figure was at the entrance to a cemetery. Both his hat and bib were clearly handmade—the former crocheted and the latter made of red cloth, faded after years of wear. I thought it was sweet that someone had taken the time to care for and dress the statue—it struck me as singular and unique. But months later, I had seen what seemed like hundreds of similarly dressed stone Buddhas in groups that ranged from six to one hundred or more. Each was dressed in the same red hat and bib. I knew that both the statue and his attire meant something, but what?

At times, the meaning of even the country's most familiar artifacts eluded me, including the ubiquitous cherry blossoms that seemed to symbolize whole tenets of the culture that were not wholly clear. I also understood little about vaguely familiar icons like the ceramic cats with waving arms placed in the windows of retail stores. I knew this creature was called *maneki neko*, but I couldn't say why so many merchants displayed them. These rich details of the landscape

Six Jizo statues lined up at the entrance of a cemetary in Horigane, Japan

were beautiful and exciting, but as exotic to my eyes as the new language was to my ears. I had come to the country with a Japanese language textbook, but I had no guide to help me see.

Unfortunately, my travel books on Japan focused on where to eat, sleep and visit, and not on the meanings of local customs and mythological creatures. While these traditional resources were helpful and informative when I needed to find a great ramen shop, they set up the travel experience as a mere checklist of things to see and do. At the other extreme of the travel book genre were the comprehensive (and typically enormous) tomes on vernacular architecture, crafts, and design—which were not suited to life on the road.

In imagining a way to bridge this gap, I started to conceive of a series of books intended for travelers and locals who wish to familiarize themselves with the everyday details that make up the soul of a place. Each book would explore the local symbols, folk art, traditions, land formations, foods—you get the idea—that are seen repeatedly throughout an environment. The series would be called "Guides for the Eyes." It has been many years now since the initial inspiration, and you are now holding the first book of the series.

Why start with New Mexico? I moved to the state from the Pacific Northwest when I was 11 years old, and much like my experience in Japan, I found the world of my new home unlike any other I had yet known. After a mild case of culture shock subsided, I quickly grew as fond of chile and as disdainful of Texas as any proud local. But after leaving the state for college and travels, I returned to find that I had never fully understood the unique imagery that surrounded me growing up. Especially for a newcomer, New Mexico's distinctive cultural geography could easily provoke the same types of questions I had in Japan.

As an area that I am already intimately familiar with, New Mexico seems to be the perfect starting point for the "Guide for the Eyes" series. My history there affords the unique ability to see the nuances of the state with the eyes of an outsider and the knowledge and love of someone who once called it home.

Incidentally, for those curious about the well cared for Buddha, I eventually learned that his name is Jizo and that he is a patron saint of travelers. But that is all I can divulge because Japan: A Guide for the Eyes is on its way.

INTRODUCTION

People have inhabited the land we now call New Mexico for thousands of years. Since European contact in the mid-1500s, Native American groups, including the Pueblo, Diné (Navajo) and Apache peoples, have witnessed new cultures flow into their spiritual homelands. Tides of newcomers through the early 1900s, including Spanish conquistadors, Catholic missionaries, archaeologists, traders, cowboys, miners, and railroad workers, as well as Eastern artists, writers, and homesteaders, saw their hopes and ambitions reflected in the territory in mingled promises of gold, Christian converts, natural resources, and land. Arriving later in the 20th century, a flow of scientists, hippies, New Agers, and other pilgrims focused on more in-tangible qualities that the landscape offered. They found inspiration, isolation, and tolerance in the sparsely populated and dramatic terrain.

This ebb and flow of migration has left behind a confluence of celebrations, flavors, textures, artifacts, and styles, which have enriched the land with icons as memorable as the state's natural beauty. This history explains the common description of New Mexico's past as a "pageantry of people" with local traditions that developed from a synergy of Native American, Hispanic, and Anglo/Western cultures. However, this simplified characterization downplays the roles that other cultural groups, such as Basques, crypto-Jews, African Americans, Asians, and Chicanos, have played in the evolution of New Mexico's complex and contested history.

With the staggering diversity of beliefs and practices represented here, it is not hard to believe that religion and spirituality are at the core of identity for many New Mexicans. Especially for Native American and Hispanic peoples, the calendar revolves around the rituals of the indigenous and Catholic religions, often performed side-by-side (and occasionally blending). Across the backdrop of these established practices is the more recent arrival of other religions and belief systems, including New Age lifestyles, enriched with Eastern philosophies such as Taoism and Buddhism.

Despite their cultural differences, the state's inhabitants have always held in common the hardships of sustaining life in a dry, unforgiving land of limited resources. However, several gifts of the earth—**corn**, beans, and squash, together with **chile**, **adobe,** and **turquoise**—have eased these difficulties and have found their way into a multitude of uniquely New Mexican expressions that are shared by all.

Chile, an iconic symbol of New Mexico, is chopped, roasted, stuffed, ground, and sauced to create many classic New Mexican dishes, from **carne adovada** to **chile rellenos**. For hundreds of years, the fruit has been a culturally significant supplement to the beans, squash, and corn that provided the basis of traditional foods. These remain essential ingredients of the state's cuisine.

Earthen housing grew out of the region's short supply of timber, abundance of sandy earth, and a need to insulate against the extremes in weather. Adobe, a mixture of sand, straw, and mud, has been shaped and styled into various forms, including **hornos**, **kivas**, and entire **pueblos**, that have become the foundations for New Mexican vernacular architecture. In some cases, the authenticity of this defining style can be debated, but adobe remains an emblem of the state.

Turquoise, with a color range from robin's egg blue to darker, moody greens, is shaped and sized into beautiful creations that include **Zuni sunfaces**, **squash blos-som necklaces**, **bolo ties**, and **fetishes**. Not surprisingly, crafts that incorporate this striking stone make popular souvenirs.

The importance of these icons to New Mexican culture showcases the harmonious connection between the land and its people. In many ways, modern technology has eased the challenges of living within this dramatic yet harsh landscape, but rustic simplicity remains a quality in all things found here (and a key aspect to the state's broad appeal). Despite our penchant for bigger, better, and faster ways of life, a step into New Mexico is an experience of beauty and timelessness that provides the calming and romantic sense that this is how it always was, and how it will always be.

ABOUT THIS BOOK

Before you begin, a few notes about the contents of this book:

- Each topic is listed categorically in the table of contents for easy reference and alphabetically on the pages to mimic their random discovery within the landscape.

- **Bold-face** words refer to another topic within the book.

- Many topics address folk traditions, which may vary greatly from region to region or even household to household. Generally, the most broadly accepted interpretations are described here.

- In respect for the indigenous groups who wish to be known by their own names, the terms Diné, Nahuatl, and Ancestral Puebloans are used in place of Navajo, Aztec, and Anasazi, respectively.

- With the exception of a few food items, all photographs were taken on location as they were found (snapshot style) with minimal or no styling.

- EyeMuse Books worked with several photographers to provide a multi-perspective view of the state. We look forward to expanding this type of collaboration for future editions of this series.

It is all very beautiful and magical here, a quality which cannot be described. You have to live it and breathe it, let the sun bake you into it. The skies and the land are so enormous, and the details so precise and exquisite that wherever you go you are isolated in the world between the micro and the macro, where everything segues under you and over you and the clock stopped long ago.

—Ansel Adams

An acequia parallels the Rio Grande in Belen, NM

ACEQUIA

Ah-SEH-kee-ah Robert Redford's 1988 movie, *The Milagro Beanfield War*, centers on a northern New Mexican village and how the impending loss of its communal irrigation ditch, or *acequia*, affects it. Through this tale that chronicles a rural farmer's fight against callous developers who threaten his right to irrigate his beanfield, the film (and the evocative 1974 book by John Nichols (1940-) on which it was based) makes a powerful case for an acequia's importance to community, and to local agriculture.

Approximately 1,000 acequias provide water to small farms throughout New Mexico. These channels are fed from rivers, such as the Rio Grande, to meet the needs of landowners along the waterline. A community-based *comisión*, headed by a *mayordomo*, or ditch boss, governs each acequia and ensures that each owner receives a fair share of the flow.

Acequias are a legacy of centuries-old Hispanic farming techniques, and remain vital—though endangered—structures within their respective communities. Threatened by development, the vicissitudes of small agriculture, and the competition for water rights in the drought-ridden West, the way of life surrounding acequias is a challenged one.

An unplastered adobe gate in Santa Fe, NM

ADOBE

Ah-DOH-beh Perhaps nothing informs the striking palette of New Mexico more than adobe architecture. Composed of clay, mud, sand, and straw, adobe has been used in different forms in the Southwest for thousands of years. In the 16th century, the Spanish introduced an adobe construction method that was likely adapted from the Moors in Spain. Here, wet adobe is formed into slab-like bricks, left to dry in the sun, then laid like masonry; the new walls are then coated with a smooth mud plaster.

Many modern buildings in the state are designed to echo historic adobe forms. Using a cinderblock or wood frame, then sprayed with weather-resistant stucco, these "faux-dobe" structures are cheap and quick to put up, but lack the innate thermal efficiency of the real thing.

True adobe walls are dense and thick; when combined with well-placed windows, they are extremely efficient in keeping heat in during the winter and out during the summer. As green building proponents revisit this and other benefits, true adobe construction, labor intensive as it is, may well prove to be an economic choice for new construction in the future. *See also Pueblo, Pueblo Ladder, Pueblo Revival Style, and Territorial Style.*

An alien mural outside the Zone II Alien Headquarters store in Roswell, NM

ALIENS

Home to a large military presence engaged in top-secret projects, it's perhaps not surprising that New Mexico has a reputation as a spawning ground for conspiracy theories and news of the weird. Among the most famous of these are the unproven claims of Unidentified Flying Object (UFO) sightings and alien encounters.

In 1947 the southeastern town of Roswell made international headlines after mysterious wreckage was found outside the city. The United States military released initial reports of a "flying disc," but officials later claimed the remnants were actually pieces of a weather balloon. These conflicting official accounts spurred intense speculation, charges of a massive government cover-up, and rich fodder for science-fiction writers.

In 1994, in an attempt to finally put an end to the unceasing interest in the matter, the Air Force released a report that concluded their story *was* a cover-up, but not for extraterrestrials. The wreckage, the U.S. military claimed, was debris from Project MOGUL, a top-secret program to detect evidence of Soviet nuclear tests. This explanation, however, hasn't quieted alien believers for whom, some 60 years later, the mystery continues.

A manmade arroyo in Albuquerque, NM

ARROYO

The thousands of dry riverbeds, or *arroyos*, that crisscross the dusty New Mexican desert help to alleviate the rush of water that accompanies seasonal rains and snow melt. But these arroyos (Spanish for "creek") are not always contained and, despite the irony, desert areas are subject to traumatic flooding. Cutting ever deeper over time, arroyos have the potential to ruin established irrigation patterns and local ecosystems. Contributing to this problem are livestock overgrazing and erosion. At its worst, arroyo cutting can reduce surrounding water tables and dump unwanted sediment on arable land (one theory posits arroyo cutting as a factor in the Ancient Puebloans' abandonment of their ancestral homelands).

Urban areas of the state, such as Albuquerque, are dependent on their arroyos to alleviate run-off; supplemental concrete-lined ditches are popular with skateboarders and bikers for their smooth, steep surfaces. However, both natural and manmade arroyos are subject to sudden, even deadly, flash flooding after heavy rainfall. Safety officials in Albuquerque created the "Ditch Witch" character and the "Ditches are Deadly" slogan to raise awareness of this danger and keep people from using arroyos for recreation. *See also Avanyu.*

A red clay pot by Maria and Julian Martinez at the Millicent Rogers Museum in Taos, NM

AVANYU

Avanyu, or "water serpent" in the Tewa language, makes its home in the Rio Grande and small waterways and springs across the Southwestern landscape. With a large plume atop its head, Avanyu is said to have a voice of thunder and a mouthful of lightning to announce the arrival of rain. Also known as *Kolowisi* by the Zuni tribe, this deity protects all sources of water, ensuring abundance for desert dwellers. As a symbol of Puebloan cultures' vital relationship with this life-giving resource, the Avanyu is invoked in the logos of the Indian **Pueblo** Cultural Center in Albuquerque, as well as the University of New Mexico Press.

The figure is believed to have orig-inated within Pecos Pueblo (now abandoned) and is commonly depicted in ancient riverside **petroglyphs** as well as on contemporary **Pueblo pottery**, especially pieces from the Santa Clara and San Ildefonso Pueblos. The latter Pueblo's most famous potters, Maria Martinez (1887–1980) and her husband Julian (1897–1943), used the rippling creature to encircle their famous black-on-black, red, and polychrome pots. Julian is said to have believed Avanyu's tail rests in Colorado, its body in New Mexico, and its head in Mexico. Today, the figure is recognized as a signature design of the duo.

A Navajo Wedding-style basket in Silver City, NM

BASKETRY

Basket-making is an ages-old craft common to most Native American groups of the Southwest. Prior to pottery-making, and dating back some 8,000 years, baskets were essential to daily life as vessels for storage, transport, and gathering the harvest.

Considered a woman's art among Southwestern tribes, basket-making skills were traditionally passed along from generation-to-generation. Mothers would teach their daughters coiling and braiding techniques using grasses, **yucca** fibers, horsehair, sticks, and reeds. Pitch was spread inside to create a watertight interior. Today, baskets are primarily made as decorative or ceremonial pieces.

The Jicarilla Apache of north-central New Mexico and the Hopi of the Four Corners area are both renowned for their fine basketry skills. Two classic Jicarilla styles are cone-shaped burden baskets, which were worn on womens' backs to collect the harvest, and tall, rounded *ollas*. The Hopi are known for the colorful coiled patterning of their flattened harvest baskets, or plaques. These are also used for ceremonial exchanges and rituals. Employing a somewhat coarser weave, Navajo "wedding" baskets are another established regional tradition.

Biscochitos from Golden Crown Panaderia in Albuquerque, NM

BISCOCHITO

Biz-koh-CHEE-toh Based on a long culinary history in New Mexico, *biscochitos* (or, *bizcochitos*) were proclaimed the official state cookie in 1989. This sugar-and-cinnamon–sprinkled shortbread was brought to the New World by Spanish explorers, along with the anise seeds that give the tasty pastries their distinctive flavor. Known as *mantecosos* in Spain, the name biscochito comes from the Spanish *bizcocho*, meaning "biscuit."

A celebratory cookie, biscochitos in the shape of fleur-de-lis are said to have commemorated the defeat of the French by the Mexican Army at Puebla in 1862, an event we now celebrate as Cinco de Mayo. To this day, biscochitos are rarely absent from holidays—especially Christmas—and other celebrations, such as baptisms and weddings. Their common shape is a simple square, diamond, or circle with scalloped edges.

Coveted family recipes, some of which include wine and other secret ingredients, are handed down from generation-to-generation. Most traditional recipes require lard, which helps to create their beloved light and flaky texture.

Dried corn cobs at Kit Carson's historic home in Taos, NM

BLUE CORN

For thousands of years, corn has been cultivated to produce various shapes, sizes, and colors. Blue corn is distinguished from yellow or white varieties by a nutty flavor, coarse consistency, and a higher protein and lower starch content. Used by native tribes in rituals and as a food source, blue corn is traditionally ground into a fine meal and made into tortillas. Today, blue corn is also a trendy ingredient of specialty goods such as pancakes, chips, and popcorn.

In New Mexico, blue corn is most associated with Arizona's Hopi tribe, who refer to themselves as "People of the Blue Corn." According to legend, when the Great Spirit presented the food to all native peoples, the Hopi made their selection but left behind varieties with greater crop yields for other tribes. The Hopi were rewarded for this generous act with a special relationship to blue corn. One use they make of this gift is their mealtime staple, *piki*—a wafer-like bread created by steaming a thin layer of blue-cornmeal batter on a hot, flat surface. *See also Corn Necklace and Posole.*

A weathered door in Taos Pueblo, NM

BLUE DOORS

Doors and window frames painted in vibrant blues is a centuries-long tradition in New Mexico. Ranging from light greenish hues to deep Prussian blue, these colors contrast beautifully against earthen **adobe**.

While the custom adds a decorative touch to regional architectural styles, its original purpose was to protect a household from bad spirits. In many regions of the world, including India, Greece, the Middle East, and Northern Africa, blue is considered a sacred, protective color, and is used in a similar manner.

This seemingly universal belief is also reflected in Native American customs, as many tribes deem that **turquoise** and other blues are revered colors of safeguarding. In colonial construction, the Spanish introduced the use of bright blue hues on doors, framing, and even roofs—a carryover from the Moorish practice of warding off the "evil eye."

Some of the best examples of this enduring practice can be found at Taos **Pueblo** and within the historic districts of Santa Fe, including the grand portal at the historic Palace of the Governors.

Deep wheel ruts lead to a corral in Arroyo Seco, NM

BLUE SKY

One of New Mexico's most celebrated features is its stunning blue sky. The state is second only to Arizona in its annual percentage of sunny days, making the ancient **Zia** sun symbol a fitting official insignia. Consistently clear skies, vast areas of low light-pollution, and low humidity (which helps the human eye see farther into the distance) have made the state a premier site for photography, stargazing, and other outdoor activities. These conditions also help to create an exceptional quality of light that has long been a draw for artists—or anyone with a keen visual sense. Many of those who have witnessed this indescribable phenomenon believe that it is not duplicated elsewhere on the planet.

Some Native American tribes believe that **turquoise** nuggets are pieces of sky that have fallen to the earth, and like the variations found among the stones, skies over New Mexico come in every shade of blue. Contrasted with earthen **adobe**, yellow *chamiso*, and green cacti, blue skies perfectly round out New Mexico's dramatic color spectrum.

A longhorn bolo worn with a bandana in Cuba, NM

BOLO TIE

The bolo (or bola) tie is the West's distinctive version of the traditional necktie. A leather cord, usually braided, is tipped with decorative metal aglets and held together with a sliding clasp—which may be simple in appearance or heavily ornamented. This accessory is so popular that both Arizona and New Mexico have proclaimed it their official state neckwear. Although bolo ties are traditionally menswear, women have recently incorporated them into their own fashions.

The most persistent tale of the bolo's origin involves an accidental discovery. In the late 1940s, Arizona silversmith Victor Cedarstaff (1905–1986) was out riding on a windy day. To protect his valuable silver-trimmed hatband, he pulled it off and slung it around his neck instead. Friends remarked on his apparent innovation, and Cedarstaff decided to refine it. He patented the concept in 1959, naming it after the *boleadora*, an Argentinean lasso with three balls at its end.

In the early 20th century Native Americans were known to wear bandanas clasped around their necks. Perhaps later Indian silversmiths were inspired by that tradition when, in the 1960s, they began crafting bolo slides of silver and **turquoise**.

Albuquerque's North Valley bosque

BOSQUE

BOH-skeh The word *bosque* is used to describe areas of rich vegetation that flourish along riverbanks in the Southwest (the name comes from the Spanish for "woodland"). Found only within these arid and semi-arid landscapes, they are havens for humans and wildlife alike.

Cottonwood, willow, mesquite, and other deciduous trees grow here, as do an unusually diverse selection of grasses, shrubs, and even lichens. The cottonwood especially has left a mark on cultural traditions of the Southwest— it has long been the wood of choice for both Native American **kachina** and Hispanic **santo** carvings.

The 200-mile stretch of bosque along the Rio Grande passes through **Pueblos**, farmland, and the city of Albuquerque. This is also the flyway for the sandhill cranes and geese that make their way south to the world-renowned Bosque del Apache Wildlife Refuge every fall. More than 377 species of birds nest at this remarkable site that the Spanish named for the tribe they encountered there in the 16th century.

Sadly, fire, development, and non-native plants are regular threats to these important bosque habitats.

A farmer's market breakfast burrito in Santa Fe, NM • Jordan Parhad

BREAKFAST BURRITO

Although breakfast burritos are found across the Southwest, New Mexicans take great pride in their own variety. Wrapped snugly inside a large flour tortilla, local ingredients may include scrambled eggs, green **chile**, potatoes, cheese, and bacon or *chorizo*. Although most fans would claim eggs to be an essential ingredient, the restaurant credited with inventing the item in 1975 (Tia Sophia's in Santa Fe) typically serves breakfast burritos sans scramble.

There are two ways to eat this satisfying comfort food: as a sit-down meal, where the burrito is smothered in a chile sauce (red or green—or both, Christmas style), or as a portable breakfast, without the sauce and wrapped up in aluminum foil. To make up for the lack of chile dressing on the latter, a healthy dose of chopped green chile is almost always found within.

These on-the-go versions are mainstays for the working crowd, and at early morning gatherings such as farmer's markets, Albuquerque's **Hot Air Balloon** Fiesta, and holiday-time **luminaria**-placing parties. Whatever way you try them, breakfast burritos are usually generously sized, filling, and, of course, delicious.

Carne adovada and warm tortillas in Albuquerque, NM

CARNE ADOVADA

KAR-nay Ah-doh-VAH-dah *Carne adovada*, or stewed pork marinated in a red **chile** sauce, was created out of necessity in the era before refrigeration. To have fresh meat last for the longest period possible without cold storage, it needs to be marinated or stewed for at least 24 hours—a time frame that essentially pickles or cures the meat. Many would agree that the longer carne adovada marinates and simmers, the more flavorful and tender the meat becomes.

Often spelled *adobada* in other regions, the New Mexican adovada variant has a long history in the state, where it is popular for many reasons. Since the dish can stew for days, it can be ready to serve at any time (this was especially helpful in territorial and frontier days, when unexpected visitors were likely to just drop in). Also, the dish is extremely versatile. It can be eaten plain, used as a sauce over other entrées, wrapped in a tortilla, or stuffed in **tamales**. And finally, pork simmered in red chile with garlic, cumin, and oregano beautifully showcases homegrown chile, the pride of New Mexico.

Ed Larson's Canyon Road studio/gallery front in Santa Fe, NM

CATTLE SKULLS

Cattle skulls are a testament to the harsh conditions of life in the desert and represent the desolation of the vast, empty spaces for which the desert is known. Georgia O'Keeffe (1887–1986) began to depict them in her oil paintings in the early 1930s, after she discovered the animal skulls during a summer trip in New Mexico. Fascinated with their weathered beauty, O'Keeffe collected skulls and other livestock bones during her solitary walks in the hills, canyons, and **mesas** surrounding Taos and Santa Fe. She even shipped her favorites to her home in New York, where she could study and paint them later. Inspired by the light and unusual beauty she found in New Mexico, O'Keeffe made the state her permanent home in 1949.

"The bones," she said of the skeletal fragments that would become icons of the Southwest, "seem to cut sharply to the center of something that is keenly alive in the desert, even though it is vast and empty and untouchable—and knows no kindness with all its beauty."

A Mesilla Valley chile field in Garfield, NM

CHILE

CHIH-leh It is difficult to fully emphasize the importance of chile to New Mexican identity and cuisine. Though technically a fruit, chile—along with **pinto beans**—is an official state vegetable that often prompts the official state question, "Red or Green?" when ordering New Mexican dishes. (Ask for "Christmas" and your dinner will come tastefully covered with both.)

Introduced to **Pueblo** Indians by Spanish explorers via indigenous Mexicans, and cultivated locally for centuries, New Mexico now has some 15,000 acres devoted to the addictive plant, most of which are grown in and around Hatch and Lemitar in the southern part of the state. Chi-

mayó, north of Santa Fe, is another center of chile production. In total, New Mexico produces about two-thirds of the chile consumed in the United States.

Chiles grow green and ripen red. A chile's flavor, shape, and heat depends on where, when, and how the pods are grown—either red or green *Capsicum* can be hottest. While red chile is typically dried and ground, the fresh green fruits are roasted and peeled. During the much anticipated fall harvest, locals revel in their charred, earthy aroma. *See also Breakfast Burrito, Carne Adovada, Chile Relleno, Enchiladas, Huevos Rancheros, Posole, and Tamale.*

Homemade chile rellenos in Albuquerque, NM

CHILE RELLENO

CHIH-leh Reh-YAY-noh The use of **chile** in New Mexico is distinguished from other regions of the world in that it is consumed as a food rather than simply a spice. Nothing showcases this better than the *chile relleno*. For this New Mexican specialty, a whole green chile (roasted and skinned) is stuffed with cheese, usually Monterey Jack or Cheddar, dipped in an egg batter, and fried. The entrée is served with its stem in place and smothered in red or green chile and cheese.

Literally "stuffed chile" in Spanish, the dish is found in many Hispanic culinary traditions. However, there are two distinctions that define New Mexican relleno style. Rather than use a poblano or dried varieties of chile, as is customary in Mexico, the long, slender, roasted New Mexican green chile is always used. Also, recipes from outside the state may use meats, spices, raisins, rice, and beans as stuffing, but in New Mexico a chile filled with anything but cheese is a rare find.

An old pickup outside the Tony Reyna Indian Shop in Taos, NM

CLASSIC PICKUP TRUCK

Whether broken down or meticulously groomed, pickup trucks are the archetypal vehicles of America. Both Ford and Dodge manufactured the first trucks in 1917; they were sold to the public for $600 to $800. Faster, cheaper, and more stylized versions followed, generating strong demand from farmers, ranchers, and small-town folk. With their large cabs and generous beds, pickups were an economic choice, serving well for both work and family life. The postwar era defined the golden age of the pickup truck, which was characterized by functional engineering, solid dependability, streamlined styling, and art deco-inspired details.

Today, mid-century American pickups—especially Chevys and Fords, such as the broad-nosed 1958 Chevy Apache 3100 and the similar 1954 Ford F-100—are highly collectible, but for many New Mexicans they are a necessity of life. The vehicles still provide a reliable means to load, haul, and maneuver across rough terrain. For some, finances might deter a vehicle update, but for others a classic truck is a proud symbol of the connection to the stark and gritty, timeless land itself.

A ladder leads to a "cavate" at Bandelier National Monument outside Los Alamos, NM

CLIFF DWELLING

For the modern sightseer, cliff dwellings offer dramatic evidence of the group of people that were long-known as the *Anasazi*, literally "Ancient Enemies" in the Diné (Navajo) language. As they were ancestors of modern **Pueblo** people, *Ancestral Puebloan* is the term preferred today.

While the Ancestral Puebloans built their homes in the open, as in Chaco Canyon, they also—perhaps for defensive reasons—took advantage of natural recesses in sheer-sided rock formations for their shelter. Inhabitants reached the often multi-story homes, which were built with sandstone or limestone, timber, and mud, via ladders or hand- and footholds etched into the stone. For exotic items, such as shells, copper bells, and parrots, they participated in a trade network that extended into central Mexico. Skilled potters who farmed the land for squash, beans, and corn, these groups thrived in the Southwest until about 1300 AD. Cliff-dwellers left their homes prior to the arrival of the Spanish and never returned.

Understandably, the ruins left by cliff-dwellers are popular attractions that provide a view into an ancient and mysterious way of life. The state's most impressive cliff dwellings are found near Silver City in Gila Cliff Dwellings National Monument, at Puye Cliff Dwellings National Historic Landmark near Española, and at Bandelier National Monument, near Los Alamos.

Vintage concho belts in Santa Fe, NM

CONCHO

The word *concho* (or *concha*) refers to both the stamped silver ornamental discs and the belts (or hatbands) they decorate. When worn with a blouse, a broom skirt, **cowboy boots,** and a **squash blossom necklace**, concho belts epitomize contemporary Southwestern fashion. This style draws inspiration from traditional Navajo attire and was popularized by the fashionable oil heiress, Millicent Rogers (1902–1953), in the 1940s.

The first conchos—which were commonly made from silver coins—appeared in the mid-1800s, shortly after Mexican *plateros* introduced their silversmithing techniques to the Navajo. The coins were flattened and thinned with a hammer, then stamped with individually cut dies to create a concho's typically intricate surface design. Eventually, cut silver sheets replaced the coins, and **turquoise** and other decorative stones were added to the hand-stamped patterns.

Meaning "seashell" in Spanish, the concho is most likely derived from a similarly shaped piece found on Spanish and Mexican bridle tacks. However, its symmetric form and stylized motifs are thoroughly Native American in origin. *See also Silver Jewelry.*

Bright corn necklaces for sale in Truth or Consequences, NM

CORN NECKLACE

Corn necklaces, made of large dried—then dyed—corn kernels strung together, come in a rainbow of bright colors and are a testament to the importance of this staple to Southwest Indians. Of their "Three Sisters" of sustenance—corn, beans, and squash—the first reigns supreme in tribal nutrition, myth, and ritual.

Corn, or *maize*, factors into **Pueblo** culture as much today as it did centuries ago. After adding an alkaline substance such as lime—to release the grains' critical nutritional element, niacin—the dried kernels are ground into a fine meal or flour.

Known as *masa*, it is the main ingredient for tortillas and **tamales**. In the past, women used stone *manos* and *metates* for grinding. Modern equipment may yield corn's bounty more readily today, but the resulting meal is still used in traditional ceremonies.

It is believed that corn arrived in the Southwest through trade with Mexico, where it was first domesticated. After thousands of years of selective breeding that began with cobs bearing but a few small kernels, early Mesoamericans eventually created highly productive crops. *See also Blue Corn and Posole.*

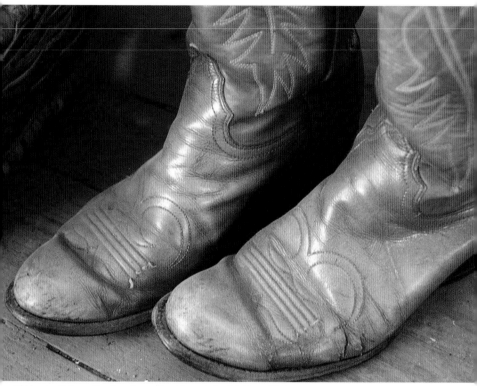

Old boots at Horse Feathers (a cowboy-themed shop) in Taos, NM

COWBOY BOOTS

Horsemen have long looked to high-legged footwear to keep their calves from chaffing and to shield them against prickly brush, harsh weather, and snakes. Out of this basic need, bootmakers of the Old West created footgear that became an icon of the American cowboy.

As more and more people headed westward in the Civil War years, it became clear that their boots—designed for military and farm use—needed some adjustment for life on the frontier. By the 1870s, custom-made boots with tall shafts, pointy toes, and underslung heels (the latter two features essential for easing in and out of the stirrup) became available.

The stars of early Hollywood westerns helped spawn a golden age for the gear. In the 20th century's opening decades, this purely functional footwear—now embellished with exotic, colorful leathers and exuberant stitching—made its debut as a pricey fashion accessory.

Today, longstanding companies such as Tony Lama, Lucchese, Justin, and Nocona supply boots in a myriad of stock styles, each marked with a signature *toe wrinkle* (a stitched decoration on the top of the toe). However, every self-respecting outfit also offers a custom fit, which many cowboys (and gals) deem a necessity. *See also Cowboy Buckle and Cowboy Hat.*

Lindsey Enderby, owner of Horse Feathers (a cowboy-themed shop), in Taos, NM

COWBOY BUCKLE

It has been said that after his horse, a cowboy's most prized possessions are his hat, boots, and belt-buckle. Not unlike their hat and boots, a cowboy's buckle is a storied treasure that is worn daily, with pride, and backed with history. The largest and most ornate buckles seen today are the trophy prizes of a rodeo or stock show. Also cherished are family heirloom buckles that may only be worn on special occasions, if at all.

Buckles are typically sterling silver, but other metals may be used for ornamentation, along with colored enamels, intricate handwork, and semi-precious stones, such as **turquoise**. However, personal adornment was not always the goal for the cowboy. This began to change in the early 1900s, as the once strictly utilitarian buckle became an obvious way to demonstrate a cowpoke's growing prosperity. And, as with their hat and boots, the accessory came under Hollywood's influence in the 1920s when leading men such as Hoot Gibson (1892–1962) and Tom Mix (1880–1940) made a fashion of their prominent buckles. *See also Cowboy Boots and Cowboy Hat.*

JB, a local of Madrid, NM, outside the town's own Mine Shaft Tavern

COWBOY HAT

Perhaps no other item has the capacity to evoke the legendary Wild West as the cowboy hat. Though worn today as much for fashion as function, the iconic hat's form evolved from the many tasks it was expected to perform. Primarily used as protection from the elements, it is also useful in whipping a horse, fanning a fire, and scooping water from a stream.

The wide-brimmed *sombreros* worn by Mexican *vaqueros* undoubtedly influenced the evolution of the American cowboy hat. In 1865 John B. Stetson (1830–1906) introduced the first style successfully marketed in the United States; he called it the "Boss of the Plains." They sold for five dollars and, like many styles today, were made from felted beaver fur. Other common materials used are straw and mink fur.

New Mexico's distinct hat style includes front-tilting creases and dents on the sides. But whatever style is favored, cowboys agree that their hat is the "the last thing taken off and the first thing noticed." *See also Cowboy Boots and Cowboy Buckle.*

A coyote eyes his observer in Chaco Culture National Historic Park in Nageezi, NM • Phillip A. Russell

COYOTE

Both feared and respected for his distinctive howl, *Canis Latrans*, commonly called coyote, is a highly adaptable animal that Mark Twain (1835–1910) described as a "slim, sick and sorry-looking skeleton [that is] a living, breathing allegory of Want." The perpetual scavenger primarily feeds on rodents and rabbits, but will devour just about anything.

As "Coyote," this skulking dog-like creature figures prominently in Native American myth. He is celebrated for his adaptability, ingenuity, intellect, and ability to provide comic relief despite his penchant for deceit, mischief, and pranks. Among the many tales that portray these seemingly contradictory characteristics, Coyote is credited with bringing fire to the first peoples, and, especially in Diné (Navajo) lore, is associated with potentially dangerous *shape-shifters* and *skin-walkers*—malevolent spirits that have the ability to morph in and out of human and animal form.

In recent decades, a new species of the coyote has emerged, one that serves as a commercial symbol of the Southwest. A fashion victim of Santa Fe–style, this variant has pastel fur, wears a bandana, and is almost always seen howling at the moon.

A coyote fence borders an adobe house in Santa Fe, NM

COYOTE FENCE

Coyote fences have long protected gardens, vineyards, and orchards from invasive predators, including the wandering **coyote** for which they are named. These structures are also used to keep animals in, serving as a corral for sheep and other livestock.

A coyote fence is a rather homespun affair; its tightly-spaced wooden posts—lengths of fallen **piñon** or juniper—are usually slim and irregular in height. (Overall, fences might stand as high as 10-feet tall.) Horizontal limbs are tacked onto the inside of the fence to stabilize the unit. The wood is very rarely peeled or smoothed, enhancing the fence's rustic look.

In non-rural areas nowadays, with privacy and local style more of a concern than grazing animals, these enclosures serve more of an aesthetic function. In Santa Fe, for example, one is more likely to see a coyote fence wrapped around a high-end **Pueblo Revival–style** home than protecting a flock of sheep.

Curandera Doña Gabrielita Pino and her apprentice, Virginia Alaniz, search for osha (a root herb) in Gallinas Canyon outside Las Vegas, NM • Lynn Johnson

CURANDERISMO

Curanderas (*curanderos* for males) are folk healers who draw upon specialized knowledge and remedies to heal physical and spiritual ailments. Practitioners are part of a centuries-old Hispanic tradition that relies on holistic treatments involving native herbs, prayer, amulets, petitions, saints, or invocations of the supernatural. The root word, *curar*, means "to heal" in Spanish.

Most practitioners become known for their abilities with particular needs: a *partera* is akin to a midwife, a *sabadero* acts as a massage therapist, and a *yerbero* is an expert on medicinal herbs. An apprenticeship is usually required to learn specific techniques as well as to develop *el don*, the God-given gift of healing.

At times, curanderismo conflicts with modern medicine. Due to the highly respected status of curanderos within their respective communities, this is rarely a problem. Outsiders have been known, though, to claim the healer's art is witchcraft. However, faith and Catholicism play an important role in the curandero's work, and to believers, all healing occurs through God. Although certain rituals would seem to conjure the supernatural, practitioners believe they can only bring about God's will.

Dreamcatchers for sale at a festival in Las Vegas, NM • Susanne Duffner

DREAMCATCHER

When placed above a bed, dreamcatchers are said to sift through the dreams of a sleeper, imprisoning nightmares in their web and allowing good dreams to pass through. Bad dreams linger in the web until morning light destroys them.

Dreamcatchers are intended for children, and are not traditionally made for long-term use. To make the spider-like web, sinew is laced around a suede-wrapped willow-branch frame. Feathers and beads may hang from the bottom, which are said to allow the good dreams to fall to the dreamer below.

Though dreamcatchers are ubiquitous today, they originated within the Ojibwe tribe of the Great Lakes area. The craft gained widespread popularity in the 1960s amidst a nationwide resurgence of interest in native cultures; they are now sold throughout the Southwest as a mass-produced souvenir.

However, handmade dreamcatchers that reflect a New Mexican touch are available, such as those created by Taos artisans, who incorporate the famous red willow for which their **Pueblo** is known.

The visitor's center at the Greater World Earthship community in Taos, NM

EARTHSHIP

With glass bottles honeycombed into rammed earth walls, futuristic Earthships have the look of a utopian vision made real. And in many ways they are. Constructed with natural and recycled materials and unconnected to city electricity or water supplies, Earthships offer inhabitants low-cost, sustainable housing that is completely "off the grid." Self-sufficiency is achieved with passive solar panels, thermal mass construction, wind harvesting, self-processed wastewater, and rainwater collection.

Mike Reynolds (1945-), founder of Earthship Biotecture, created the first Earthship in 1989 outside Taos.

Dozens of Earthships now dot Highway 64 outside the town in Cerro de Taos, most of which belong to the Greater World subdivision, an alternative housing community.

Earthships—which have made some inroads around the globe—are only one of the latest advancements in a long tradition of alternative architecture in New Mexico. Equally influential techniques and projects which were born or developed over the last 50 years in this arid land of abundant sun include geodesic domes, zomes, trombe walls, and of late, the nation's first straw-bale post office and bank-financed straw-bale home.

New Mexican homestyle stacked enchiladas made with fresh red chile from Chimayó, NM

ENCHILADAS

Across the greater Southwest, *enchiladas* commonly arrive at the table rolled in groups of two or three. In this variation of the dish, corn tortillas are filled with cheese, chicken, beef, or pork, then covered with a **chile** sauce, a sprinkling of cheese, and perhaps some raw onion, and baked. Although this rolled variety is common in restaurants, homemade versions in the state are usually served up differently.

New Mexican homestyle enchiladas begin with the same lightly-fried corn tortillas, perhaps of the **blue** corn variety. These are stacked about three deep, with red or green chile, cheese, diced onion, and occasionally meat layered in between. The whole dish is then smothered in more chile and cheese for good measure, and baked as a casserole. Some families top the dish with a fried egg.

The word enchilada translates to "in chile," which is an appropriate term, whether tortillas are rolled or stacked. Regardless of the style tried, only one rule applies: Mom's version is always best.

Wonderstone Bear fetish by Dinah & Peter Gasper • Courtesy of Keshi, the Zuni Connection

FETISH CARVING

Fetishes are miniature stone carvings thought to embody the unique powers of the animals they represent. The Zuni people, who are most closely associated with this craft, have a pantheon of animal spirits used as fetish symbols, each with their own strengths. For example, those in need of courage and power may call upon the medicine bear—one of the most popular fetish carvings—or in times of a drought, a frog may be invoked. As a talisman, a fetish is carried around, put on display, or kept in a clay pot. In order to reap their benefits, fetishes must be cared for and respected, with the occasional feeding of cornmeal, for example.

Simple in nature, fetishes are usually carved from local stone, jet, or **turquoise**, and are often tied with an offering of tiny arrowheads, and shell, coral, or turquoise beads. Some animals also have *heartlines*. These are zigzag incisions—often inlaid with turquoise or silver—that extend from the mouth to the heart area to represent the spirit's path of breath.

Traditional flan with caramel sauce

FLAN

Flahn *Flan* is a sweet custard dessert that readily found a place in New Mexican cuisine after being introduced to the region by the Spanish. Made with simple ingredients typically on hand at ranches and farms—including eggs, whole milk, and sugar—its creamy texture and rich flavor is also enjoyed throughout areas of Mexico and Latin America.

Served cold, flan is baked with hardened caramelized sugar at the bottom of a baking dish; when it is baked or steamed through, the dish is flipped over and the flan is released for serving. The cooking transforms the underlying sugar glaze into a golden-liquid topping for the soft dessert.

Flan's comparable cousin, *crème brûlée,* is distinctly characterized by a rigid caramelized topping, and is often served warm. Both desserts are usually cooked in individual ramekins, although flan is presented on a separate serving dish.

A slightly lesser known, but similar custard-style dessert of New Mexico is *natillas*. Using different proportions of the same flan ingredients, natillas is a richer, softer custard that lacks caramel sauce, but is topped with a healthy sprinkling of powdered cinnamon.

A traditional hogan near Torreon, NM • Jordan Parhad

HOGAN

In the Four Corners region of the state, the traditional houses of the Diné (Navajo) dot the landscape. While styles vary across time periods and are influenced by available materials, a hogan almost always opens to the East to greet the sun, and is most commonly a one-room circular structure built of wood and mud (and sometimes stone). Most also have a hole in the roof, to allow smoke from an interior fire to escape. Because the Diné people would typically abandon a dwelling after the death of a family member, or to move on to new graz-ing areas, hogans are not necessarily built to be permanent structures.

There are two types of hogans: male and female. Male hogans are used for ceremonies and tending to the sick; the female hogan is a center of domestic life. This is where a family eats, cooks, sleeps, and gathers. Though these structures are still a common sight in northwestern New Mexico, most hogans built today are for ceremonial purposes; relatively few Navajo considered them a primary dwelling by the late 20th century. *See also Sand Painting.*

A cluster of small-scale hoodoos in the Bisti Badlands/De-Na-Zin Wilderness Area • Larry Lamsa

HOODOO

New Mexico has been subject to voluminous volcanic activity for millions of years. Some of the resulting volcanic fields and *calderas* (a basin or crater where a volcano collapses) contain striking rock formations known as "hoodoos." Their strange and evocative shapes are created when the soft rock that lies beneath a harder cap rock is eroded away by wind and water. Typically tall, thin pedestals topped by oddly shaped boulders, these unexpected formations can make the surrounding landscape more akin to Mars than Earth. Some hoodoos are known by their anthropomorphic shape, such as Tesuque's Camel Rock, which can be seen from I-5 just north of Santa Fe.

Two well-known areas of the state offer exceptional showcases of these natural sculpture gardens: Kasha-Katuwe Tent Rocks National Monument, southwest of Santa Fe, and De-Na-Zin Wilderness Area (also known as the Bisti Badlands), south of Farmington. However, the state's northwestern San Juan Basin contains several lesser known, but just as spectacular, badland areas that are worth the time and energy to find. Amid the Dali-esque scenery, wanderers can ponder the ages of time in stratified layers of ancient sediment, dinosaur and early mammal fossils, petrified wood, and shiny obsidian pieces called "Apache Tears."

Well used hornos in Taos Pueblo, NM

HORNO

In the backyards of most Indian **Pueblo** homes are freestanding beehive-shaped ovens called *hornos*. Pueblo women build their hornos by hand with mud-plastered **adobe**, fuel them with **piñon** or cedar, and use them to bake staples ranging from puffy oven breads, cookies, and fruit pies (*pastelitos indios*) to corn, vegetables, meat, and puddings. After a fire has been built inside the horno, the embers are removed when an ideal temperature has been reached. Long-handled wooden paddles are used to transfer the shaped doughs and other foodstuffs in and out.

Prior to European contact, tribes made cornmeal-based breads, such as Hopi *piki*, in dugout ovens or by flattening the dough onto well-heated slabs of rock. Wheat came with the Spanish, as did the methods for building and using the horno. Over time a variety of Indian breads emerged that can still be bought outside Pueblo homes or on the roads leading to each Pueblo. Among many specialties, Jemez Pueblo is patronized for whole-wheat bread and Zuni for tangy sourdough loaves.

Balloons at the Red Rock Balloon Rally in Gallup, NM • Alex Cashman

HOT AIR BALLOON

Fall is arguably the most beautiful time of the year in New Mexico, and it is made even more so when a fantastic spectacle is on view. On the cool mornings of the first two weeks of October, colorful balloons of every shape and size speckle vibrant blue skies as part of the International Balloon Fiesta.

What began in 1972 with a 13-balloon launch from a shopping-mall parking lot has grown into the largest event of its kind in the world. Close to a million spectators gather annually in Albuquerque's Balloon Fiesta Park to watch more than 700 balloons take off, sometimes all at once. The Balloon Glow, where balloons gas up simultaneously at nightfall, is another spectacular Fiesta event.

Albuquerque, the state's largest city, has more resident balloonists per capita than anyplace else on the planet. But, it isn't the only spot in New Mexico to fly. With its large, open spaces and consistently clear weather, the state offers enough prime launch locations—as attendees at popular rallies in Gallup, Farmington, and Taos can attest—to make any balloon fan ecstatic.

A huevos rancheros breakfast at the Frontier Restaurant in Albuquerque, NM

HUEVOS RANCHEROS

WAY-vohs Ran-CHAIR-ohs *Huevos rancheros*, or simply *"huevos,"* is a traditional New Mexican breakfast dish. The entrée is made with poached, scrambled, or fried eggs on top of a fried corn tortilla, all of which is smothered in **chile** and cheese. Beans, and sometimes *papas* (small cut-and-baked potatoes), are typically served on the side.

Originating in Mexico, huevos rancheros is Spanish for "Ranch Eggs," denoting a country-style breakfast served midmorning to ranch hands following a smaller meal at dawn. Along with so many other customs from Mexico, it is thought that Mexican kitchen staff, families, and ranch workers brought the dish to the Southwestern United States.

For New Mexicans, it's all about the chile. Whether smothered in red chile, green chile, or a mixture of both (called "Christmas"), the dish is sure to satisfy any appetite.

Pueblo Maiden Queen and Pueblo Chief King glass panels at The Buffalo Thunder Resort and Casino in Santa Fe, NM • Courtesy of the artist, Michele Tapia-Browning

INDIAN CASINO

In 1997, after ten years of negotiations with state tribes, New Mexico legalized tribal-owned casinos. What began as little more than high-stakes outdoor bingo tents has morphed into a sophisticated industry, providing a huge economic boost for Indians and their surrounding communities. Today, 14 pueblos and tribes run 24 casinos across the state, offering gaming from bingo and slots to the high-roller's baccarat. Services and amenities range from basic buffet-style restaurants to resort hotels, spas, big-name live entertainment, and golf courses. Five of the "Vegas on the Rio Grande" complexes (not all Indian owned) have racetracks—these are cutely known as *racinos.*

Although controversial, Indian nations are allowed to operate casinos because their sovereignty is recognized by the federal government. However, unlike commercial gaming, in which owners may enjoy all profits, New Mexico law requires that a portion of revenues from tribal-owned facilities goes to community purposes, such as housing, education, or health services. Slot machines alone earn tribal casinos over $500 million dollars in annual revenue; 8 percent of that amount goes to the state.

A "Tewa Taco" in Las Vegas, NM • Susanne Duffner

INDIAN FRY BREAD

Indian Fry Bread is a sinfully delicious snack food most prevalent in the Four Corners region of the state. As its name implies, the food is simply a flattened round of fried dough. Like funnel cake, its greasier and sweeter cousin, fry bread is a well-loved staple of fairs, pow-wows, markets, and family gatherings.

Some vendors top their fry bread—which is akin to the **sopaipilla** in its preparation—with a myriad of toppings, including onions, lettuce, tomatoes, **chile**, beans, cheese, and ground beef or shredded lamb to make a heavenly (and some would say irredeemably carb-heavy) meal called the "Navajo Taco." Although many tribes offer this taco variant using the name "Indian Taco," the Navajo have special claim to the dish. They conceived it during their 1863–1868 internment at Bosque Redondo where the federal government provided them with meager rations of flour, yeast, salt, and sugar, which they soon learned to mix together and fry in lard.

Though a relatively recent culinary development, Native Americans consider the puffy bread a traditional food that provides a unifying thread throughout their diverse cultures.

A stuffed Jackalope on display at the Jackalope store in Albuquerque, NM

JACKALOPE

The Jackalope is an antelope and jack-rabbit hybrid said to live throughout the American West. According to legend, the creature was first spotted in 1829 in Douglas, Wyoming—the self-proclaimed Jackalope Capitol of America. Resident Douglas Herrick popularized the figure by selling mounted Jackalope heads to the pubic in the 1930s. Although the figure has since been regularly featured in Western novelty postcards, its profile has been elevated in New Mexico through the popularity of an eclectic home and garden store of the same name.

Folktales claim the creature has the ability to mimic the human voice—helpful in playing tricks on cowboys around a campfire. Others claim the Jackalope is a species of killer rabbit that may be trapped with a whiskey bait. Despite the far-fetched stories, some truth exists in the lore of this strange crossbreed. *Shope Papilloma* virus, which affects rabbits, produces branch-like growths that often resemble antlers. This condition, first studied in 16th century Germany, likely inspired stories of horned rabbits in America and Europe.

A collection of kachina dolls in Albuquerque, NM

KACHINA

Kah-CHEE-nah **Pueblo** tribes believe that all things in nature—including plants, animals, and mountains—possess a spirit being, or *kachina*. The word, sometimes seen as *katsina*, refers to three different entities: the supernatural beings; the dancers who impersonate the beings; and the corresponding hand-carved and painted wooden dolls.

Hundreds of diverse characters make up the kachina pantheon, which is most dominant in the Hopi and Zuni cultures. According to myth, kachinas once lived among humans, but left to live in the mountains after feeling disrespected. Every winter kachinas return to the pueblos and stay until midsummer, during which Pueblo tribesmen honor them with celebrations and dances and beseech them for rain and plentiful harvests. On dance days, specially (and secretly) groomed boys and men don the sacred kachina costumes through which they are believed to (briefly) become the individual kachinas they represent.

Also at dances, females and young boys are given kachina dolls as part of their training in tribal religious beliefs. Once used solely for this purpose, they are now popular collectibles, providing carvers a source of income and an outlet of artistic expression. *See also Kiva, Koshare, and Zuni Sunface.*

An underground view of a kiva at Pecos National Monument in Pecos, NM • Jordan Parhad

KIVA

KEE-vah Kivas are unique to **Pueblo** tribes. Their name is derived from the Hopi word for "ceremonial room." Every kiva has a dedicated membership, typically decided by clan. Primarily a male bastion (women may enter on certain public occasions), men gather here for socializing, but also to perform such sacred tasks as initiation rites, **kachina** dances, and religious ceremonies.

Historically, kivas were circular and built below ground, but today many are rectangular and constructed above grade. As with a traditional Pueblo dwelling, a kiva is entered from its roof; this entryway is also where smoke exits from a kiva's interior fire pit, or hearth. Also inside are plastered and painted walls, a ventilation shaft (to draw in fresh air), **nichos**, *bancos* (built in seating), and a small hole, or *sipapu*. Dug directly into the earth, a sipapu is said to symbolize the first realm of human existence, the site from which native ancestors emerged from a lower world. (In this Puebloan system, the kiva's floor represents a second realm, bancos the third; the fourth is the world we live in today.) *See also Pueblo Ladder.*

A kiva fireplace keeps a room warm in Taos Pueblo, NM

KIVA FIREPLACE

Kiva fireplaces are commonly found in traditional **adobe** and **Pueblo** homes, as well as contemporary **Pueblo Revival**, or "Santa Fe-style" houses. Also called beehive fireplaces, they were introduced to the Southwest by the Spanish. Prior to their arrival, open hearths built into the floor in the center of a room provided heating. The smoke they created would be drawn out via the same hole in the roof used for an entry ladder. In contrast, kiva fireplaces—usually set in a corner of a room—allow for smoke to exit via a chimney. Until gas heating became common-place, such fireplaces were a primary source of heat throughout the region. Their presence today—at least in upscale designer homes—may be purely decorative.

Kiva fireplaces, old and new, are often flanked by *bancos*, which are built-in benches. Like **nichos**, bancos are usually formed along with the walls and then covered with the same smooth plaster coating. Bancos and nichos are two elements that are also found in actual kivas—the ancient ceremonial chambers of the Pueblo people.

Kokopelli decorates a wall in Gallup, NM

KOKOPELLI

Kokopelli is an ancient figure recognized by many tribes in the Southwest. A humpbacked flute player with protrusions on his head, Kokopelli represents music, dance, fertility, rain, and harvest. He is active in the domains of agriculture and childbirth, chasing winter away and carrying seeds and babies on his back, the latter of which he distributes to women.

While depictions of Kokopelli first appeared in Hohokam pottery as far back as 850 AD, and are quite common in **petroglyphs** found throughout the region, his image is even more ubiquitous today. The musical fertility figure has caught on as a general representation of the Southwest, and may be found on everything from yard art to T-shirts. Although this contemporary image is emasculated, Kokopelli, like many fertility gods, was drawn in the past with a distinctively large phallus.

Scholars cannot confirm early Native American artists' inspiration for the popular character, but speculations range from roaming Aztec traders to the desert robber fly. This promiscuous insect, called *pelli* in Hopi and Zuni, has a prominent proboscis and a notably rounded back.

A painted gallery sign features a Koshare in Gallup, NM

KOSHARE

Koh-SHAR-ree Among the **kachina** dancers of the **Pueblo** and Hopi people are boisterous creatures known as *Koshare*. These beings portray negative human behavior to exemplify how *not* to act in Pueblo culture, and are instantly recognizable for this lack of social grace, as well as their distinctive appearance. Broad black and white stripes decorate their bodies from head to toe, while two similarly striped horn-like appendages, each topped with colorful corn plants, stick up from their heads.

Thought to arrive from the clouds, Koshare (who are also known as Hano Clowns) descend upon villages at dance time, making their presence known by prancing across rooftops and broadcasting booming announcements. Their trademark comedy routine begins when they clumsily fall to the ground below.

During a dance, the Koshares are spontaneous, riotous, rude, and laugh-inducing. They play tricks, perform physical jokes, and engage in an embarrassing and disrespectful manner with the crowd. This seemingly light-hearted behavior is used to reinforce cultural taboos and teach tribal morals. To showcase their gluttonous nature, they carry watermelon slices, a typical prop of the popular Koshare kachina carvings.

Rosalia de Aragon prepares for the lead role in the play 'Cuento de La Llorona/Tale of the Wailing Woman,'
written and directed by Rosa Maria Calles • Courtesy of Rosa Maria Calles

LA LLORONA

Lah Yor-OH-nah La Llorona, or Weeping Woman, is the memorable main character in a classic Hispanic folktale that is echoed in literary traditions around the globe. Perhaps you are familiar with its tragic theme: La Llorona drowns her children in a river, and is consumed with grief. Unable to rest, she is heard at night pacing the river's edge, crying and moaning for her loss.

Most New Mexican towns have their own twists on the tale. In some, she is portrayed as a harlot, having killed her children to free herself for a lover. Others explain the drownings as revenge for a husband's or lover's betrayal. Another account marks La Llorona as a victim; in this version, she is forced to drown her cherished children to spare them from a worse fate.

Always, La Llorona is recognized by her flowing black hair, white dress, and eerie wailing. To keep themselves from her icy clutches, children across the state are told not to play by a river or wander outside at night.

Joyriders at a lowrider rally in Española, NM • Bob Snead

LOWRIDER

A lowrider is essentially a vehicle that, thanks to an altered suspension, rides much closer to the ground than a standard model. Owners spend tremendous amounts of time and money adding colorful paint jobs (typically featuring Catholic imagery), fancy rims, lush upholstery, powerful stereos, and bouncing hydraulics. But more than simply a customized car or truck, a lowrider is a canvas for artistic expression and ethnic pride.

Española, in north-central New Mexico, is considered the birthplace of the state's lowrider subculture and claims to have more lowriders per capita than anywhere else in the world. The Smithsonian gave weight to the claim when the museum inducted a lowrider from the city into its collection in 1990 as an important artifact of folk culture.

Two theories explain the origins of this American tradition. From a New Mexican perspective, lowriding evolved from the old Mexican custom of parading horses along *paseos*. However, enthusiasts in Los Angeles, another hotbed of lowrider culture, believe the movement grew from a desire for a clear Chicano identity in post-WWII America. At a time when speedy hot-rods were jacked high off the ground, Mexican American youth chose vehicles that were Low and Slow (*Bajito y Suavecito*)— perfect for cruising slowly down the main drag in town.

"Electro-litos" on a restaurant rooftop in Las Cruces, NM • Louis C. Vest, OneEighteen Photography

LUMINARIA

Lou-mihn-AH-ree-ah *Luminarias* bring a warm glow to one of the longest evenings of the year. A uniquely New Mexican Christmastime tradition, these small parcels of light line pathways, rooftops, and ledges in glowing tranquility. The tradition began in the 16th century with the small bonfires, also known as luminarias, that lit a traveler's way to midnight mass on Christmas Eve. Today, votive candles are placed inside small brown paper bags that are weighted down with sand; they are believed to illuminate a path for the spirit of the Christ child to enter a household.

In Santa Fe and other points north of Albuquerque, these lights are known as *farolitos*, or "little lanterns." Like strings of Christmas lights, luminarias are proudly displayed on homes in many neighborhoods. On town churches and plazas, setting up elaborate displays is a serious community endeavor involving thousands of lights. And, in tourist areas, electric luminarias, known as *electrolitos*, stay up over the course of the Christmas season. Especially beautiful in the snow, luminarias reflect the wonder of the season.

Corn Mesa near Zuni Pueblo, NM • Renée Ann Wirick

MESA

MEH-sah The highly respected—and decidedly colorful—frontier journalist, Charles F. Lummis (1859–1928), once referred to New Mexican *mesas* as "islands in the sky"—a fitting term for these isolated and seemingly random landforms. With level tops and steep inclines on one or more sides, mesas understandably derive their name from the Spanish and Portuguese word for "table." These dramatic oddities are created when the top layer of a plateau resists the natural weathering process. As the softer deposits around the more durable cap-rock erode, a mesa forms.

Some Native American people, such as the Acoma, have taken advantage of these sheer-sided formations for strategic, defensive purposes, settling temporary or permanent villages atop them. Resting some 350 feet above ground level, Acoma **Pueblo** (also called "Sky City")—which for many centuries was accessed only by a staircase cut into the mesa's sandstone sides—prompted one 16th century Spanish conquistador to call the settlement "the best situated Indian stronghold in all Christendom."

Decorative milagros for sale in Santa Fe, NM

MILAGRO

Milagros are metal charms that are most commonly held as personal amulets (called *dijes*) or presented as an offering to a particular saint. As offerings (also known as *ex-votos*), believers leave milagros in churches and shrines to solicit help with a troubling matter or as a token of gratitude for an answered prayer.

Translated as "miracles," milagros are cast-molded and produced in multiples from tin or pot metal, or custom-crafted in pure silver. Their generally small, flat form easily fits into the palm of a hand. Milagros are made in the likeness of humans, animals, or objects that are meant to represent the object of their petition. Human body parts, such as hearts and arms, are especially popular; an eye might be selected to petition for better eyesight, a heart for mending a soured romance.

Today, milagros play an active role in modern Catholicism throughout the Hispanic Americas, but especially in Mexico, where Spanish missionaries first introduced the European custom.

San Francisco de Asis Mission Church in Taos, NM

MISSION CHURCH

Scattered throughout the state, but concentrated along the Rio Grande Valley, are the built remains of the Franciscan friars who accompanied Juan de Oñate (1552–1630) on his journey north from Mexico in 1598, when he was sent to colonize Spain's new territory. Of the more than 20 Catholic missions the Franciscans established in New Mexico over the next two centuries, a number still survive—notably those in use today at Acoma, Laguna, and Isleta **Pueblos**.

Along with a new religion, the Spanish introduced European industry, livestock, and produce, as well as foreign diseases, unrelenting religious and cultural intolerance, and forced labor (including for mission-building itself). The inevitable Pueblo Revolt of 1680 sent the colonists into exile; it was the only successful Native American uprising against Europeans in the United States. Twelve years later, though, the Spanish returned to the Pueblos and the missionary work resumed.

Despite the Franciscan attempt to subsume Indian religious practices, Native American culture has survived, blending in many Catholic traditions along the way. Nothing exemplifies this better than feast days—public celebrations of the namesake saint of each Pueblo.

An historic morada at El Rancho de las Golondrinas outside Santa Fe, NM

MORADA

Moradas lie quietly among the chapels and churches of the old Hispanic villages of northern New Mexico. These modest, one-story **adobe** buildings are the meeting houses of the Los Penitentes Hermanos (The Penitente Brothers), a lay society of Roman Catholic men. Although they are often difficult to locate and in poor condition, morada structures can still be found in Truchas, Taos, Mora, and Abiquiu.

The Penitentes established themselves in New Mexico during the Spanish Colonial era (1598–1821) and flourished after Mexican church leaders began to expel Franciscan priests from the Territory in 1790. Through the next century, Los Penitentes presided over many community and priestly duties at a time when no other priests were available to do so. Many credit them with the preservation of Catholicism in New Mexico amidst a void of official Catholic authority.

The group's extreme religious practices, including self-flagellation, bloodletting, and mock crucifixion, were performed publicly, most notably in the days leading up to Easter Sunday. These displays inspired intense public scrutiny and media intrigue, prompting Catholic authorities to condemn the acts in 1889. Since that time, the Penitentes have functioned as an underground organization.

*A Nambé artisan with a handcrafted metal alloy bowl in Santa Fe, NM •
Courtesy of Nambé*

NAMBÉ

Nahm-BAY Nambé has designed and manufactured handcrafted goods for the home since 1953, when the company was established in the Tewa-speaking **Pueblo** village of the same name, just north of Santa Fe. Nambé is a Tewa word meaning "people of the round earth."

Nambé's most celebrated and established products are made from a patented eight-metal aluminum-based alloy created at Los Alamos National Laboratory in the 1940s. As the exclusive producer of such goods, the company guards the secret production process closely, and they have reason to do so. Exceedingly functional, Nambé metalware retains both heat and cold and resists tarnish. The material is as "solid as iron" and has a high polish luster, despite the fact the alloy contains no lead, silver, or pewter.

Nambé takes great pride in its award-winning, signature design sense, which is marked by smooth, organic, and asymmetric forms. The company frequently collaborates with distinguished designers, such as Eva Zeisel (1906–) and Karim Rashid (1960–), to create these elegant, timeless, and durable vessels.

Handmade cloth dolls in Farmington, NM

NAVAJO CLOTH DOLL

The simplicity of a hand-sewn doll is irresistible in any culture and is no less so in the Diné (Navajo) tradition. Since the late 1800s, tourists have gravitated towards these souvenirs, which showcase the traditional Navajo dress that is still worn today for ceremonies, and as daily wear for some elders.

This distinctive dress style was adopted from Anglo women's fashions of the mid-1800s following the Navajo internment at Bosque Redondo from 1863 to 1868. (This was the infamous period in Indian history known as the Long Walk, when the United States government forced over 10,000 Navajos and hundreds of Apaches off their land and relocated them to Fort Sumner, 300 miles away.)

At Bosque Redondo, Diné women learned to sew from army wives and came to admire their jewel-colored velveteen blouses, calico prints, and long, tiered skirts. They would later complement this attire with a shawl and **silver jewelry**. This new style of dress replaced traditional cinched-waist blanket wraps and affected menswear as well, which also came to include velveteen shirts, moccasins or leggings, jewelry, and a headband.

A vintage "eye dazzler" style rug in Taos, NM

NAVAJO RUG

According to Navajo myth, Spider Woman used sunshine, rain, and lighting to teach weaving to the Diné (Navajo) people. The craft evolved thanks to the exceptional skills of the Diné women who practiced it, as well as the techniques they learned from **Pueblo** and Hispanic artisans, who had weaving traditions of their own. The Pueblos introduced vertical looms to the Diné around 1650 and the Spanish later contributed Churro (a sheep prized for its fine fleece), striped-pattern techniques, and natural indigo dye.

By the turn of the 19th century, traders were acting as middlemen between the Diné and tourists. With their knowledge of Anglo preferences, traders had tremendous influence on the colors and motifs the Navajos would use. Well-known designs such as Ganado and Two Grey Hills are still known by the trading posts that encouraged them. Traders also effectively switched the weavers' emphasis to rugs instead of blankets, which had been in demand in frontier days for their watertight finish.

All fine Navajo weaving has long commanded high prices, compensating both its artistry as well as the many hours devoted to each creation. Today, some of the most rewarding purchases are made at the monthly Crownpoint Navajo Rug Auction in the Four Corners region, where collectors may buy straight from the artisans themselves.

A bulto (santo carving) displayed in a nicho in Albuquerque, NM

NICHO

NEE-cho First found in the Southwest in the **kivas** of the Ancestral **Pueblo** people, *nichos* are recessed shelves created in the process of **adobe** wall construction. Traditionally, sacred objects such as **fetishes** and other talismans were placed inside them. After the Spanish arrived in the New World, these features were incorporated in adobe constructions as altars for religious icons, such as **santos**. During the Spanish Colonial era (1598–1821) travelers adopted portable nichos. Made from wood or tin, these painted and decorated sacred cabinets could easily be displayed, then packed up again.

As a modern-day architectural detail, nichos are extremely popular in southwestern-style homes for the display of saints, personal keepsakes, artwork, religious mementos, or other revered—or mundane—objects. To allow for the best viewing of these displayed works, nichos are typically installed at eye level in the walls around a home or above a **kiva fireplace**.

Researchers investigate details of an astronomical simulation in the Cave Automatic Virtual Environment (CAVE) at the Los Alamos SuperComputing Center • LeRoy Sanchez

NUCLEAR SCIENCE

New Mexico rushed into the modern era in 1942 when the U.S. government appointed the remote camp of Los Alamos as headquarters for the top-secret Manhattan Project. It was here that scientific luminaries such as J. Robert Oppenheimer (1904-1967) worked feverishly to create an atom bomb. Three nuclear devices were developed, one of which was tested on July 16, 1945 at the Trinity Site within the White Sands Missile Range. Less than one month later "Little Boy" and "Fat Man" were dropped on Hiroshima and Nagasaki.

These historic beginnings led to the creation of Kirkland Air Force Base, and the world-renowned Sandia and Los Alamos (LANL) National Laboratories, which have been cru-cial to national defense projects since the Cold War. The state is also home to other weapons research labs and storage areas, explosives testing sites, a uranium enrichment plant, America's largest radioactive spill site, and the controversial Waste Isolation Pilot Plant (WIPP), the nation's only major nuclear waste disposal facility.

For anti-nuclear activists like Ed Grothus (1923-2009), the founder of the quirky Black Hole weapons surplus shop in Los Alamos, New Mexico's involvement in nuclear activities is a disgrace. However, for tens of thousands of workers in the field, nuclear science has introduced money, jobs, historic significance, and a sense of pride in areas that might otherwise still be lonely **mesas**.

A tile mural at the Santuario de Guadalupe in Santa Fe, NM

OUR LADY OF GUADALUPE

Our Lady of Guadalupe is the most revered patroness in all of New Mexico and a vibrant symbol of Hispanic culture. She has been inextricably linked to the hearts and minds of her devotees ever since her first appearance, to Juan Diego outside Mexico City in 1531. At that miraculous moment, *Nuestra Señora de Guadalupe* spoke to Juan Diego in his native Nahuatl (Aztec), and requested that a church be built on that very site. As a proof of her appearance, she later asked Juan to pluck the roses that inexplicably bloomed before him despite the dark December day. He se-cured them in his *tilma*, or poncho, onto which her image once again appeared upon his presentation of the lush red flowers to a bishop.

For such miracles she is fervently venerated, most visibly on her December 12th feast day, and especially in northern New Mexico where many small *santuarios*, shrines, and wall murals are devoted to her. Her image, pervasive even in mainstream culture, attests to the key role she plays in Hispanic Roman Catholicism, making it difficult to imagine the religion without her.

Richardson's Pawn Shop in Gallup, NM

PAWNSHOP

Lining historic districts around the state are the brightly colored and often kitschy signage of pawnshops. But it is on old **Route 66** in Albuquerque and Gallup, and up in Farmington—all places touched by the trading common to Indian Country—that they have the richest history.

There is evidence that native peoples of the region and those from afar have always traded with each other to obtain needed goods. That trade expanded with the arrival of Hispanic explorers and colonial settlers, but it wasn't until Anglos arrived in the mid-1800s that trading posts and "Indian Pawn" were introduced to New Mexico.

The system itself is simple: a person in need of money brings valuable items, such as rugs or jewelry, to a pawnbroker or trading post. The shop owner provides cash or provisions in return for the opportunity to sell the items—hence the marketing of "Indian curios." Trading-post owners won their good reputation, however, when they would hold a family's precious silver and **turquoise** until they had the funds—or substitute pawn—to redeem it themselves. Controversial as less scrupulous operations may be, dealing in pawn is an institution in New Mexico, and is not expected to disappear anytime soon.

The bright designs of a Pendleton blanket in Albuquerque, NM

PENDLETON BLANKET

Blankets have long been important for Native Americans, providing warmth, shelter, and even status. Although many tribes had well-established weaving traditions, Indians began acquiring machine-made blankets by the late 19th century as a matter of convenience—at least for simply staying warm. Soon referred to as "Indian trade blankets," they became so highly valued that, like pawn jewelry, they were used as a standard of money in exchange for other necessities at trading posts across the Old West.

Pendleton Woolen Mills, founded in 1889, endures as one of the most well-known manufacturers of this commodity. Their signature geometric designs, both colorful and intricate, are an important component of their vast success. Pendleton designers gathered information from tribes across the country to determine the preferred motifs of their market. The company continues to produce these popular American icons out of Portland, Oregon.

Pendleton blankets are still commonly seen as raffle prizes at powwows, or wrapped around the shoulders of jewelry-makers selling their wares and Indian men prior to a dance. Although Indians themselves, especially the Diné (Navajo), are celebrated for their fine hand-weaving skills, these lush mass-produced textiles are also an enduring symbol of their culture. *See also Navajo Rug.*

Rock art at Petroglyph National Monument in Albuquerque, NM

PETROGLYPH

Petroglyphs are carved-rock images that are thought to number in the tens of thousands in New Mexico. The term is derived from the Greek words *petros*, meaning "stone," and *glyphein*, "to carve," because petroglyphs are made by scraping or chiseling the dark patina off a rock's surface to expose lighter material underneath. Petroglyphs are distinguished from pictographs, which are prehistoric images that are painted onto a rock surface.

The petroglpyhs found in New Mexico date back to about 2,000 BC.

Starting in the 17th century, Spanish colonizers also left marks, most notably at Inscription Rock in what is now El Morro National Monument. These religious symbols and signatures are fairly straightforward. However, most other petroglyphs in the state are Native American in origin and range from spirals to representations of humans and animals; these are harder to decode. No one knows for certain whether they hold sacred or astronomical meaning, act as guides, or simply indicate a human presence at a point in time.

Roadside piñon trees in Santa Fe, NM

PIÑON TREE

PEEN-yohn Speckling the hills among the junipers, the *piñon* is the beloved state tree of New Mexico. Its timber provides *latillas* and **vigas** for building, and its logs and saplings fuel many a woodstove and fireplace, adding a comforting aroma to cold winter nights.

In fall, the trees are shaken to release sweet pine nuts onto blankets below, and roadside vendors with fresh piñon crops dot rural roads and highways. Eaten roasted and salted, and even ground into coffee for a uniquely New Mexican flavor, piñon nuts were considered "better than those of Castille" by the early Spanish explorer Cabeza de Vaca (~1490–1557), who gave the tree its common name. Still savored, piñon nuts remain expensive delicacies; the trees only produce large quantities of pine nuts every seven years and there is no mechanized way to pick or shell them.

A native to North America, *Pinus edulis*, as the piñon tree is scientifically known, grows in Colorado, Utah, and Arizona, but is most abundant in the high desert of New Mexico, in elevations ranging from 5,500 to 7,000 feet.

Pinto beans and green chile at the Owl Cafe in Albuquerque, NM

PINTO BEANS

Along with squash and corn, beans are one of "Three Sisters" that comprise the traditional food staples of the **Pueblo** people. Native Americans, along with nearly every early settler of New Mexico—from Franciscan missionaries to Hispanic ranchers—owed their strength to this nutritional powerhouse. And, while sufficiently healthy alone, the dietary value of beans increases exponentially when they are combined with corn, greatly reducing the need for more costly protein sources. For its long legacy in the state's culinary history, the pinto bean, along with **chile**, is one of New Mexico's official vegetables.

Pinto beans have a distinctive speckled skin, which inspired their Spanish name, *frijol pinto*, or "painted bean." The prepared beans, called *frijoles*, turn a dusty pink color and are traditionally served whole, but the mashed "refried beans" are also popular. (The term "refried beans" is a mistranslation of *refrito*, meaning "really fried," and not fried twice, as the name implies.)

Regardless of the manner they are served, the bean's infamous ability to produce intestinal gas is well known. Chefs minimize this effect by adding a bit of *epazote*, an herb also known as Mexican Tea, to the cookpot.

Multicolored posole ready to be cooked in Hatch, NM

POSOLE

Poh-SOH-leh In New Mexico, *posole* refers to both a traditional stew and hard kernels of field corn that have been boiled in a lime solution to remove the germ. This centuries-old process, called *nixtamalization*, was invented by Native Americans and allows the body to better absorb corn's vitamin content. This step in the preparation of corn as a food is crucial in preventing the potentially deadly niacin deficiency called *pellagra*.

Posole, often spelled as *pozole* in other regions, is simmered with pork and **chile** to produce a type of stew served across the American Southwest and Mexico. There are a mul-titude of variations, categorized by three styles—red, green, and clear. To make this classic dish, many cooks substitute a similar product called hominy for posole because it tends to be easier to find. However, posole kernels are usually preferred for their rich, earthy flavor.

Prepared as this hearty stew, posole is also New Mexico's traditional Christmas Eve meal. In the Hispanic villages of northern New Mexico, it may be served after "Las Posadas," a community reenactment of Mary and Joseph's search for lodging prior to the birth of Jesus. *See also Blue Corn and Corn Necklace.*

New growth on a prickly pear cactus in Albuquerque, NM

PRICKLY PEAR CACTUS

One of the most widely distributed cactus plants in New Mexico, the prickly pear is easily recognized for its broad paddle-like segments, thin sharp spines, delicate flowers, and deep-pink berries. This native plant is part of the genus *Opuntia*, which consists of more than 200 species.

The prickly pear is unique in that it produces flowers, berries, *and* a vegetable. The berries, called *tuna* in Spanish, can be eaten raw or may be juiced for use in candy, drinks, and jellies. Its pads are also edible and are sold as a vegetable called *nopales*. Long savored by animals and hu-mans alike, both tuna and nopales are nutrient-packed sources of vitamins, minerals, and fiber. Scientists are currently investigating claims that the plant carries cholesterol lowering, immune boosting, and blood-sugar stabilizing properties.

Prickly pear cacti have many protective features. Their pads can each detach, grow roots, and form new plants. They also have two types of potentially nasty prickles: long, sharp spines as well as tiny barbed hairs, or *glochids*, which can severely irritate one's skin.

Afternoon sun on Taos Pueblo in Taos, NM • Jordan Parhad

PUEBLO

When the conquistadors came upon New Mexico's indigenous villages in the 16th century, they called them *Pueblos*, Spanish for "town." Missionaries soon named many of the individual Pueblo towns—and so, the people inhabiting them—after Catholic saints. For a handful of the state's 19 Pueblos, these names, including Santo Domingo, San Felipe, and Santa Ana, remain.

Pueblo people are a diverse group who do not all speak the same language, but their separate tribes do historically have in common farming, pottery-making, the celebration of **kachina** spirits (noted with other words for some tribes), and a unique architectural style.

Most Pueblos developed around a central plaza; **kivas** and residences alike would be clustered together in massed earthen or stone apartment-like complexes. Most early Pueblo rooms were small and many traditional activities took place outdoors, often on the flat rooftop.

Today, not all Pueblos are readily open to the public. However, two equally accessible Pueblo destinations that offer impressive insights on Pueblo architecture and cultural heritage include Taos, a UNESCO World Heritage site, and Acoma, also known as "Sky City." *See also Pueblo Ladder and Pueblo Pottery.*

A ladder lays against an adobe wall at Taos Pueblo in Taos, NM

PUEBLO LADDER

In a land of earthen houses and isolated **mesas**, tall hand-hewn ladders are yet another touch of exoticism for travelers in New Mexico. These sky-piercing constructions have served as reminders for visitors—from Spanish conquistadors to 20th century artists—of the unique ways of life to be witnessed here.

Historically, a **Pueblo's** multistory dwellings did not have ground-level doors; they could be entered only from an opening in the roof. Ladders would be left outside, resting against the structure's outer wall, ready for its residents to clamber up or down. This system is thought to be defensive in nature: a ladder could be quickly tucked away in the event of an attack.

In the modern context, Pueblo dwelling construction today usually includes standard swing-style doors. However, ladders are still used to enter or exit **kivas**. In some Pueblos, kiva ladders are made to be especially wide and have 3 support poles, to distinguish the sacred chamber.

In contemporary settings, ladders are simply decorative, serving as indicators of trendy Southwestern style. Though they lead to nowhere, the rungs are popularly used to showcase other regional crafts, such as Indian blankets and rugs.

A polychrome clay pot by R. Boren of Acoma Pueblo, NM

PUEBLO POTTERY

Among many other attributes, Ancestral **Pueblo** people are known for their long tradition of pottery-making. Their sedentary lifestyle, based on agricultural subsistence, led to the development of pottery for daily functional uses, such as cooking and storage, as well as for ceremonial purposes.

Pottery-making methods and their classical forms have changed little over time. Women still gather local clay, then temper it with shards of broken pottery. Pots are hand-built with a coil-and-pinch method, and burnished with stones or corncobs to produce a soft luster. They are then hand-painted with natural mineral pigments and fired outdoors.

Although surface decoration can trace a pot to a specific Pueblo, there is much innovation today, and with it, cross-pollination of design ideas. Maria Martinez (1887–1980) of San Ildefonso, famed for her black pottery decorated with matte black designs, laid the groundwork for modern Pueblo pottery. Among other traditional modes seeing variation today are polychromes; micaceous ware (made with clay infused with mica); and redware. *See also Avanyu and Storyteller.*

The inner courtyard of the New Mexico Museum of Art in Santa Fe, NM

PUEBLO REVIVAL STYLE

Pueblo Revival architecture—New Mexico's iconic building form—evolved in the early 1900s as Anglo-American tastemakers sought a unique identity for the state. The style borrows heavily from historic Pueblo and Spanish Colonial building traditions, and is characterized by the use of earthen hues, hand-hewn woodwork, including **vigas** and *latillas*, parapet walls, sturdy massing, soft edges, and organic lines. But the form's defining features are often simply surface imitations of their muse, built as they usually are from concrete block or frame rather than traditional **adobe**.

While the style may be found throughout the state—the legacy of the WPA projects of the 1930s—Pueblo Revival architecture is largely associated with John Gaw Meem (1894–1983). The University of New Mexico in Albuquerque has an impressive concentration of his work, dating from 1933 to 1959, when he was the school's official architect. And this is, of course, the predominant style in Santa Fe. Meem was influential in establishing the "City Different's" zoning laws, which prescribe Pueblo Revival or **Territorial styles** for all new buildings there—hence the moniker "Santa Fe style."

A Queen Anne style house in Las Vegas, NM

QUEEN ANNE STYLE

For many people, Queen Anne-style architecture epitomizes the Victorian-era house. The style is immediately distinguishable from the state's ubiquitous streamlined and stuccoed **Pueblo Revival-** and **Territorial-style** buildings with its colorful brick-and-shingle construction, wraparound porches, steeply pitched roofs, turrets, and gables, all assembled onto asymmetrical façades.

Unrelated to any royal figure, Queen Anne architecture is based on the work of English architect Richard Norman Shaw (1831–1912), and arrived in New Mexico in the 1880s with the **railroad**. As railcars rolled into upstart frontier towns, residents gained access to previously unavailable construction materials, including bricks and precut lumber. The new style took off, and was often completed without the aid of architects, as generic plans had also become readily available.

While it fell out of favor as a building style by the early 1900s, Queen Anne style homes are still found in many areas of the United States. New Mexico has some superb examples, notably in communities that took hold only after the arrival of the railroad, such as Las Vegas and Silver City.

The sun sets over tracks in Lordsburg, NM

RAILROAD

In 1878 the Atchison, Topeka, & Santa Fe Railroad (AT&SF) laid tracks in New Mexico as part of an effort to connect Denver to Mexico City. Impenetrable passes deterred a full realization of this plan, and while Albuquerque got service, Santa Fe did not (until a spur from Lamy was later built). While the "City Different" survived, other missed communities declined. A town's inclusion on a line resulted in an influx of products and people, and with them, a wealth of new ideas and cultural influences.

The railroad also inspired the nation's first chain restaurant operation. Introduced by Fred Harvey (1835–1901) in 1876, his eponymous Harvey Houses served travelers all along the Santa Fe line. By the 1880s, the high-quality restaurants dotted the route at 100-mile intervals; hotels were added at the busiest stops. One such site was Santa Fe's La Fonda Hotel, which still welcomes guests today.

The AT&SF—now operating as the Burlington Northern Santa Fe Railway—is also still in service; while passengers no longer make the journey, it continues to play a vital role in the transport of the nation's goods as a freight line. *See also Queen Anne Style and Tin Roofs.*

A road sign depicts a rain motif surrounded by a stylized rainbow in Los Lunas, NM

RAIN CLOUD MOTIF

Just as moisture is vital to life in a dry, hot land, the rain cloud is an indispensable motif common to almost every Native American tribe in the Southwest. It is rendered on pottery, rocks (as **petroglyphs**), **kiva** walls, and **kachina** dolls. It not only represents the desire for rain, rain itself, or cloud presence, but may also act as a symbol of renewal, fertility, or change. For some clans, the rain cloud motif represents their family line.

With an average rainfall of barely 8.9 inches per year, the need for water is a serious concern in New Mexico. (Arizona and Nevada are the only states with lower annual rainfall.) Much of New Mexico's annual rainfall occurs in the months of July and August, a period known as "monsoon season." During this time, large rain clouds will quickly move in on an area, darken the sky, unleash heavy rainfall, and, just as quickly, move on to do the same in another locale. For most drought-stricken residents, this natural ritual is a welcome one.

Brewer Ranch in Capitan, NM

RANCH GATE

A fine, tall gate makes for a grand entrance to ranches large and small across the rural acres of New Mexico. While each ranch gate reflects the whims (or pomposity) of the respective ranch owner, they all share a few basics: two tall support beams stand on either side of the entrance drive, and the crossbeam that joins them typically identifies the owners. But it's the unique personal touches, such as wooden carvings and wrought-iron silhouette sculptures incorporating family names and cattle brands, that make these Western icons stand out.

Ranching is big business in New Mexico; dairy products, cattle, and calves alone account for three-quarters of the state's agricultural commodity sales. While cattle country primarily lies south of Albuquerque, the state's largest ranch lies in a northeastern spread and contains no cattle. Owned by the famously nonconformist media mogul Ted Turner (1938–), the historic 590,823-acre Vermejo Park Ranch now functions as a corporate retreat and a reserve for bison, pronghorn sheep, elk, and other wildlife.

Autumn ristras for sale in Hatch, NM

RISTRA

REE-strah Whether hung to add a little color, or in keeping with a centuries-old tradition, a bright, red string of **chiles** is a familiar feature at the entrance of homes across the Southwest. While many of the *ristras* made today are used purely for decoration, the custom is based on the longtime method employed to dry chiles for use in the kitchen. (Another technique, often seen in chile production areas of the state, is to lay the fruits on the flat roofs of houses to dry them in the sun.) Chiles dried on a ristra can be enjoyed up to a year after harvest without refrigeration.

Plucked from a ristra a few at a time, they are typically ground into a powder to make a red sauce.

Ristra means "string" in Spanish—and that's the key to how a ristra is formed. The most common method in New Mexico is to tie the fresh plump pods in clusters of three onto a cotton string, which in turn is wound onto a heftier support twine or wire.

Nu-Mex Big Jim and New Mexico #6 chile varieties are ristra favorites. For a slightly different look, the smaller Pequin chiles are used for mini-ristras and wreaths.

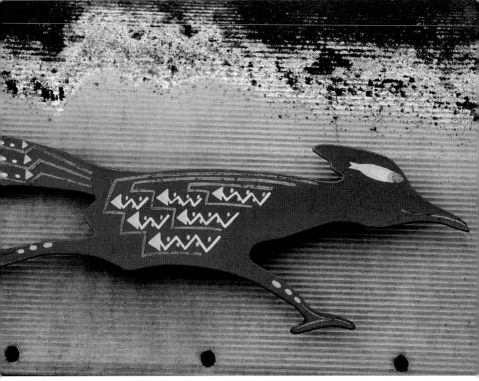

A roadrunner mailbox flag in Silver City, NM

ROADRUNNER

The roadrunner, also known as the chaparral bird, is the state bird of New Mexico. With strong legs, short wings, and a distinctive head crest, the bird is best known as Wile E. Coyote's archenemy in Warner Brothers cartoons. As his name implies, rather than fly, the roadrunner prefers to let his legs scoot him across the desert, where he reaches running speeds of up to 17 mph.

Native to the southwestern United States and northern Mexico, the roadrunner is well suited to the desert. An omnivore, he lives off seeds, fruits, rodents, insects, lizards, and snakes (even rattlers!), gathering moisture from a great range of foods. During the midday heat the bird lays low, saving his energy for the cooler evening. His unique physiology, which allows salt to be excreted efficiently through his nasal passages, provides another cooling benefit.

Though generally solitary birds, roadrunners are known to live in pairs. They have a lifespan of about seven or eight years.

A descanso placed between the Rio Grande and Highway 68 in Embudo, NM

ROADSIDE MEMORIAL

Descansos (Spanish for "resting place") are roadside memorials that mark the spot of an unexpected death. Family members and friends usually erect these shrines within days of a tragedy to pay tribute to their loved ones. As with gravesites, descansos are faithfully tended to and are often considered holy ground—the place where a soul departed. They range from simple white crosses to elaborate shrines embellished with flowers and other personal mementos.

Once unique to the American Southwest and Mexico, roadside memorials are now found across the continent. While many states limit the practice, in New Mexico it is a respected folk tradition with roots in early Hispanic Catholicism. Scholars believe the practice can be traced back to the custom of marking the spot where pallbearers in a funeral procession paused to rest. With the arrival of the automobile, a similar tradition evolved along roads and highways as a stark reminder of life's fragile path.

Signage for El Don Motel on Central Avenue (old Route 66) in Albuquerque, NM

ROUTE 66

Referred to as the "Mother Road" by the author John Steinbeck (1902–1968), Route 66 spans 2,448 miles from Los Angeles to Chicago. Opened in 1926, the road was part of a larger initiative to open highways across the continental United States. Millions of travelers used this historic two-laner as a route to their destination or as part of a journey all its own. Its popularity gave rise to countless mom-and-pop establishments and one-of-a-kind roadside attractions, including kitschy curio shops and novelty motels. In 1946, Bobby Troup (1918–1999) immortalized this uniquely American experience in his classic song, "(Get Your Kicks on) Route 66."

While it originally cut north into Santa Fe, a realignment tinged with local political intrigue dropped the road down to an all east-west route in 1937. In New Mexico, the highway meanders through Gallup, Albuquerque, Santa Rosa, and Tucumcari, though Interstate 40 officially replaced the storied byway in 1985. While remnants of Route 66 remain—and are well-signed—I-40's current route bypasses the ever-shrinking small towns that were once busy with travelers passing through.

Sagebrush in Golden, NM

SAGEBRUSH

Sagebrush is a hardy, evergreen shrub with a natural habitat ranging from western Canada south into Mexico. Its pervasive presence in sandy, sunny areas of New Mexico makes it a key source of food for desert animals (though it can be toxic to cows and sheep); for humans, it is widely known as a medicinal herb. In Spanish it is called *Chamiso Hediondo*, or "stinking sagebrush," for its distinctive odor. The plant's leaves can be brewed to make a tea used for battling colds, fevers, and indigestion. Native Americans also use sagebrush in ceremonies as a cleansing and purification agent because the herb promotes sweating. Despite its numerous healing properties, however, sagebrush is a primary hay-fever irritant throughout the western states.

True sagebrush is often confused with rabbitbrush, known locally as *chamisa* (also *chamiso*). Both plants have silvery greenish-gray leaves and display yellow blooms in early fall. However, the scientific name for sagebrush, *Artemisia tridentata*, is helpful in its identification. The plant's distinctive three-lobed leaves inspired the name *tridentata*, meaning "three teeth." *See also Smudge Stick.*

A sand painting for sale in Gallup, NM

SAND PAINTING

The Diné (Navajo) people believe in a concept called *hozho*, which, roughly translated, means "beauty" and "balance." When an individual's hozho has been disrupted, illness can occur. This imbalance is corrected with songs, rituals, and sand paintings.

In North America, sand painting is most associated with the Diné, although a form of this spiritual art is also found in the Tibetan tradition. The Diné refer to this delicate art as *iikaah*, "a place where the gods come and go," because in their creation, Holy People are invoked to help restore balance or preside over a blessing.

A Navajo medicine man makes a sand painting by distributing naturally-colored substances, such as sand, pollen, and crushed flowers onto a **hogan** floor in a symmetrical composition of symbols and stylized images. Upon completion, the patient is placed upon the sand painting and left to soak in its power; afterwards, the images are destroyed.

Due to their sacred content, genuine sand paintings are not available to the public. However, in the 1940s, artists began crafting versions of the artwork for tourists. These works use non-ceremonial imagery and are rendered with crushed rock and sand glued onto a firm board. *See also Yei.*

*A bulto in a **nicho** at the Iglesia de la Virgen de Guadalupe in Velarde, NM*

SANTO

SAHN-toh *Santos*—depictions of Catholic saints—are holy objects that are either paintings (*retablos*) or sculptures (*bultos*) for use in both churches and in homes. The tradition is grounded in Spanish Catholicism, and was brought to the state by the early missionaries.

Retablos, meaning "behind the altar," were more or less replaced by mass-produced prints in the late 1800s. However, santo artisans, or *santeros*, such as Taos artist Patricino Barela (1900–1964), have revived the craft of bulto carving in recent decades. As with generations past, santeros use cottonwood or pine, and may carve the saint in sections, which are then joined with dowels. A completed bulto may be painted with natural mineral pigments or left to its natural finish.

Both antique and contemporary santos of New Mexico are characterized by a rustic simplicity that reflects the Spanish Colonial period (1598–1821) in which the craft was established in the Americas. Due to the isolation of the northern villages in which they lived, santeros of that time had little access to sophisticated tools and had to lean on their own imaginations when rendering a saint and his symbolic attributes. *See also Nicho.*

A Diné (Navajo) woman outside her home near Cuba, NM • Jordan Parhad

SILVER JEWELRY

Although Native Americans have a long history of jewelry-making, the signature silver creations for which they are now renowned developed relatively recently.

Atsidi Sani, "Old Smith," is credited as the first Navajo silversmith. He learned the trade from Mexican *plateros*, or silversmiths, in the mid-1800s, about the same time silver was discovered in the state. Initially though, silver was sourced from melted coins. As the craft was passed on to the **Pueblos**, native-made jewelry, fueled by the demands of tourists and other non-native art collectors, became an important trade item as well as a significant source of income.

Among many distinct styles, the Navajo are best known for combinations of **turquoise** and silver, often employing casting or die-stamp techniques, while the Zuni are masters of intricate petit point, and the Santo Domingo are famed for their inlay work.

Native American jewelry makers certainly take cues from past traditions of their cultures, but their continual innovations keep this evolving craft alive. The stunning array of jewelry available in galleries, as well as displayed by the artists themselves on the plazas of Santa Fe and Albuquerque, is an impressive showcase of their artistry.

Smokey Bear notifies passerbys of low fire danger in Capitan, NM

SMOKEY BEAR

Smokey Bear (sometimes incorrectly referred to as "Smokey *the* Bear") is the familiar mascot of the longest running public service announcement in American history. Dressed in jeans and a campaign hat and armed with a shovel, the beloved Smokey character was introduced in 1944 as part of a WWII-era effort to help protect American forests. At the time, these valued resources were considered vulnerable to both foreign attack and domestic carelessness. Smokey followed on the heels of Bambi's successful stint as the country's first animal chosen to champion fire safety.

In 1950, a real cub rescued from a human-ignited fire in southeastern New Mexico's Capitan Mountains was adopted as the living embodiment of Smokey. Little Smokey, who suffered burned paws and lost his mother, was flown to the National Zoo in Washington, D.C., where he lived until his death in 1975.

Today, Smokey Bear (whose slogan was switched in 2008 to "Get Your Smokey On" from the venerable "Only You Can Prevent Wildfires!") is considered the most recognizable fictional figure in the United States after Santa Claus. He is buried at the Smokey Bear Historical Park in Capitan, New Mexico.

Smudge sticks for sale in Taos Pueblo, NM

SMUDGE STICK

Smudge sticks are a simple assembly of dried stems and leaves that are bundled together to form a wand. Many types of herbs and shrubs may be used, but white sage, **sagebrush**, and cedar are among the most popular.

Burned to banish bad spirits, influences, thoughts, and sickness, the flowering end of a stick is lit so that its burning embers release a pungent smoke, which is believed to purify and cleanse a surrounding area. After a user wafts the stick through the air, it is left on a plate to burn. The lingering smoke is thought to attract the negative presence in a space, then carry it away as the smoke dissipates.

The use of smudge sticks is a long tradition of Native American cultures, particularly of Southwestern tribes. Once used only in native ceremonies, New Agers far and wide have adopted the tradition as a step toward spiritual cleansing or simply as a calming ritual that is built around the smudge stick's comforting, earthy aroma.

Lunch time sopaipillas at Jerry's Cafe in Gallup, NM

SOPAIPILLA

Soh-pah-PEE-yah A distinguishing part of any New Mexican meal is the tempting *sopaipilla*. Akin to little pillows, sopaipillas are light, air-filled fried breads made of triangular or rectangular pieces of dough.

Sopaipillas in New Mexico generally come with your main course; the honey that accompanies them is a perfect salve when the **chile** gets too hot. Sans honey, and stuffed with an assortment of meat, cheese, chile, beans, tomatoes, and lettuce, they are sometimes offered as an entrée in their own right.

Sopaipillas are thought to have originated as part of Hispanic cuisine in the Old Town section of Albuquerque in the late 1700s. The name likely comes from the Spanish, *sopaipa*, which translates to sweet fried dough.

Although the ingredients used to make sopaipillas are similar to those for **Indian Fry Bread**, many say the secret to their extraordinarily light and puffy nature is in the handling of the dough. Sopaipilla dough is rolled out, then cut into shape; the fry bread mixture is hand-formed into small rounds.

A vintage squash blossom necklace from Traders' Collection in Santa Fe, NM

SQUASH BLOSSOM NECKLACE

Distinguished by a large crescent-shaped pendant hung from a chain of gracefully fluted silver beads, the squash blossom necklace is a distinctive style of Native American jewelry. The design of the necklace itself is Navajo in origin, although the inverted central crescent motif, or *naja*, has roots in the Middle East, where it is believed to protect its wearers from the "evil eye."

The naja form traveled with the Moors to Spain, then with the conquistadors to Mexico, where it was used in silver bridle and trouser ornaments. As Navajo jewelry-making evolved under the influence of Mexican silversmiths, the tribe in-corporated the naja into their own traditions of horse ornamentation and personal jewelry.

The fluted beads may resemble the native squash blooms for which the necklace is named, but many believe their shape emerged from the pomegranate blossoms of Spain, which in turn traveled to the Americas via the Spanish. The Navajo word for the necklace, *yo ne maze disya gi*, translates simply to "bead that spreads out."

Early squash blossom necklaces were made purely of silver, but today **turquoise** is added to enhance the appeal of this spectacular adornment. *See also Silver Jewelry.*

St. Francis welcomes guests to a gallery shop in Chimayó, NM

ST. FRANCIS

St. Francis (1181–1226) of Assisi, Italy, is a Catholic saint remembered for his great compassion and love of all living things. For this he is the patron saint of flower growers, animals, birds, and the environment, and is commonly depicted in garden statues and **santo** carvings. Often portrayed within a circle of birds, St. Francis is also traditionally shown with his hair cut in a tonsure and wearing a brown robe tied with a knotted rope. The rope's three knots symbolize his three virtues: poverty, chastity, and obedience. However, New Mexican *bulto* carvings (three-dimensional santos) often show him hooded, with a beard but no tonsure, and with his robe tie lacking the three knots.

The saint has special importance in New Mexico. Due to the many Franciscan friars who settled here in their quest to bring Catholicism to the New World, the state was once called the "New Kingdom of St. Francis." Several Franciscan communities remain in the state today.

St. Pasqual and St. Anthony are two other Franciscans commonly invoked in New Mexico. St. Pasqual, the patron of cooks, is typically found in the kitchen (somewhat plump from the tasty treats he finds there). St. Anthony, the patron of missing things, is recognized by the white lilies and baby Jesus he holds. According to folk tradition, he is also called upon to help in affairs of the heart, much like St. Valentine elsewhere.

Storyteller by Dennis Anderson of Cochiti Pueblo, NM

STORYTELLER

With eyes closed and mouth open, ceramic storyteller figures sing songs and tell stories to children who listen intently. While these hand-painted clay figures came into vogue but 40 years ago, they are formed with ancient techniques and honor the long oral tradition of their cultures.

Helen Cordero (1915–1994) of Cochiti **Pueblo** created the first recognized storyteller in 1964. Her frustration with making more traditional jars and bowls led her to experiment with figurative subjects, and Alexander Girard (1907–1993), the influential folk art collector and designer, encouraged her work. After he requested a seated figure, she made a likeness of her grandfather; joined by five children huddled close by, they listen raptly as he tells them a story.

The storyteller was a significant innovation in the history of figurative pottery-making at Cochiti, a tradition which includes "singing mothers," animals, and caricatures of visitors to the New World. A still-evolving form, native artists from Cochiti and other Pueblos—notably Acoma and Jemez—continue to explore the storyteller theme. *See also Pueblo Pottery.*

Decorative Talavera tile in Santa Fe, NM

TALAVERA TILE

With rich patterns in blue, white, yellow, green, and brick red, Talavera tiles bring a vibrant warmth to hotels and restaurants, plazas, and homes throughout New Mexico. Whether employed as a simple accent or covering an entire wall, they always make for an eye-catching display.

Talavera pottery is a form of *majolica*—earthenware that is hand-painted over an unfired tin glaze. Its signature paint colors are produced from mineral pigments, which help distinguish genuine Talavera work. Historically, use of the color blue—a pigment ground from lapis lazuli—was mandated by code, as the semiprecious stone's high cost would discourage fakes.

The style originated in the 13th century, in Talavera de la Reina, Spain; it was brought to Mexico three centuries later by Spanish guild artisans who were retained to decorate the then-new Catholic churches. The name Talavera today refers to the eponymous tiles, which are now made in Mexico, mostly in the town of Puebla. Artisans there still employ 16th century techniques, resulting in a unique blend of tradition, manufacturing processes, and styles of the old world and the new.

Tamales for sale at a Plaza kiosk in Santa Fe, NM

TAMALE

Tah-MAH-leh Not many people can resist the steamy package found inside the tightly wrapped corn husks of a *tamale*. Enjoyed long before the arrival of Columbus, the name for this traditional Native American food comes from the Nahuatl (Aztec) word, *tamalli*. An early version of a sandwich, tamales were likely developed as a portable ration for traveling warriors.

In New Mexico, tamales have since been adopted as an Hispanic tradition, served for special occasions such as weddings, baptisms, Christmas, or Easter. Recipes are handed down from generation to generation and, like *pierogies*, are best made in large batches with a group of people. This time-consuming endeavor begins by smearing *masa* (a cornmeal-based dough) onto one side of a flattened corn husk. A dollop of filling is placed on top and the husk is wrapped around it for steaming. Although a combination of red **chile** and pork is standard filling fare, less conventional choices, such as cheese, pumpkin, or fruits may also be found.

A Territorial-style building at Sena Plaza in Santa Fe, NM

TERRITORIAL STYLE

"Territorial" is a regional building style that flourished during New Mexico's tenure as a United States territory (1846–1912). An adaptation of the indigenous **adobe** architecture that was then prevalent, it was influenced by the Greek Revival trend that had become popular in the East. These fresh ideas arrived along with window glass and sawmill equipment on the wagons that inaugurated the Santa Fe Trail in 1821.

Low-slung with simple geometric forms, and distinguished by an austerity of detail, Territorial stands in distinct counterpoint to the later **Pueblo Revival style**. With newly available milled lumber, traditional Spanish and Pueblo *portales* got a bit of neoclassical embellishment. Local brick from Civil War–era kilns was used for protective coping atop adobe parapets. Pitched roofs—built to shed snow and rain—were added. Trim was painted white, and as all-brick construction caught on, served in pleasing contrast to the darker masonry or adobe walls.

Territorial architecture readily took root in frontier strongholds such as Lincoln County, down El Camino Real, which ran south from Santa Fe into Mexico, and along the Santa Fe Trail itself. *See also Tin Roofs.*

A humble adobe dwelling in Madrid, NM • Jordan Parhad

TIN ROOFS

In most areas of the state, **adobe** and adobe-style structures feature a flat roof. Historically made with packed dirt (tar is the more common surface today) and surrounded by a low parapet wall through which *canales* drain off excess water, these roofs are vulnerable to collapse from the extra weight heavy rains and accumulated snowfall can bring.

Prior to the late 1870s and the advent of the **railroad**, this was a particular problem in the mountainous regions of the state. But soon, new building materials—such as corrugated metal, which was previously un-available in isolated outposts—came pouring in on trains from the East. Residents quickly took to these galvanized sheets, propping them together to create A-frame roofs from which snow and rain could easily be shed.

Built onto a traditional adobe or **Territorial-style** home, these pitched tin roofs are a defining feature of Northern New Mexico style architecture, though they are found elsewhere as well. Multiple stories, exposed rafters, long portals, and tall windows characterize this unique adaptation, also called Western Victorian.

A tin chandelier at Pecos National Monument in Pecos, NM

TINWARE

Known as "poor man's silver," tin is highly malleable, inexpensive, and resistant to corrosion, making it an ideal material for crafts. The tradition of tinware crafts in New Mexico represents a huge array of decorative and functional items ranging from elaborate framed mirrors, candelabras, and altarpieces, to simple votive holders and small frames.

When imported British tinplate became widely available in the Southwest in the 1820s, the tinware industry in New Mexico flourished. Flat sheets could be cut, pressed, shaped, punched, pierced, or embossed with patterns to make functional and decorative products. Also, tin cans could be easily re-formed into shadow-throwing candleholders and sconces.

Although Anglo tinsmiths introduced new tin-shaping methods to the region in the early 19th century, tinware largely remains a Hispanic craft. The heavily Catholic aspect of this heritage is expressed in common tin items, such as crosses, church ornaments, and frames for the popular devotional prints that replaced original *retablo* paintings of the saints in the late 1800s.

A tumbleweed roundup in Dixon, NM

TUMBLEWEED

Seen rolling across a barren plain, tumbleweeds are the quintessential metaphor for Western mythology. Selected to symbolize a rootless, solitary lifestyle, the plant has starred in movies, songs, and literary lore. And, like the cowboys they emulate, tumbleweeds are relative newcomers to the West. The plant first landed on American shores in the 1870s, arriving in South Dakota from its native Ukraine via a shipment of flax seeds. The tumbleweed's other common name, *Russian Thistle*, indicates the shrub's original habitat.

With small yellow flowers and even smaller green leaves, the plant is innocent-looking enough when first sprouting. But as the seasons pass, the plant dries out and literally tumbles away, leaving its taproot behind to sprout again. Carried by the whim of the wind, the noxious plant can travel far afield, scattering its seeds everywhere it goes.

Today, the tumbleweed is viewed as a destructive, invasive weed. But despite their prickles and tendency to pile-up in river beds or snag on fences (or bombard a moving car), New Mexicans find that with a shot of white paint come winter, the stacked-up tumbleweeds make a fine Southwestern-style snowman.

Turquoise bead strands at a jeweler's supply store in Santa Fe, NM

TURQUOISE

Turquoise has been mined in New Mexico for many centuries. For Native Americans, it has long been an important material for ritual, trade, and decoration. One of the oldest turquoise mines in North America is in Cerrillos, just 25 miles south of Santa Fe. A popular, though debated, theory holds that the Cerrillos mine was the Aztec empires' source for the semi-precious gem.

Although the Spanish eschewed turquoise in their quest for gold, later Mexican, and then American prospectors mined here, including Tiffany & Co. Not unlike other artisans who covet turquoise for its striking variations in color and webbing, Charles Lewis Tiffany (1812–1902) sought perfect light blue stones to showcase in his jewelry. Ranging from pale blue to murky green, the mineral's appearance depends on how much iron (green) or copper (blue) it contains.

Once the country's largest source of turquoise, Cerrillos has produced very little since the 1920s. Today, most turquoise used in Native American **silver jewelry** comes from Nevada, Arizona, and China, and may be treated to enhance or strengthen the soft material; only stones labeled "natural and untreated" are truly unadulterated.

Playful vigas and latillas on the ceiling of the historic Mabel Dodge Luhan House in Taos, NM

VIGA

VEE-gah *Vigas* are large wooden logs that are laid horizontally across structural walls to create a ceiling and support a roof. Often massive, these beams are typically left exposed in interior rooms and are purposefully cut to project beyond a building's outer walls. (Some scholars believe this exterior feature came about from a functional necessity: foodstuffs such as **chiles** or meat could be safely hung, out of reach of predators, to dry or cure.) In the past, the particular wood used for vigas was determined by the closest available source, which often meant a long trek into the mountains.

Additional wood was collected for *latillas*. These peeled saplings are laid snugly side-by-side atop the vigas, filling the space between them. Whether laid in a herringbone pattern or placed perpendicularly, their light color often provides a striking contrast with the usually darker-colored vigas.

Vigas are key features of Native American building traditions that were adopted and popularized by early Spanish settlers. Still used widely, vigas remain an integral element of New Mexico's distinct architectural styles. *See also Adobe.*

A towering Yei statue outside a recreation center in Gallup, NM

YEI

Yay Gracefully tall and slender, *Yei* figures are images of Diné (Navajo) holy beings. Imbued with the power to cure, they are invoked for healing ceremonies and are often depicted with symbolic plants and a rainbow on which they travel. Round heads denote male yei; their female counterparts have rectangular heads.

When rendered face-on, Yei figures represent the beings themselves, while side-facing figures are dancers impersonating the Yei, and are known as *Yei'bi'cheii*. Yei'bi'cheii participate in healing ceremonies that take place during the winter months to bring back the health of sick individuals.

Once seen only in **sand paintings** and ceremonies, Yeis and Yei'bi'cheii are now commonly featured in pictorial **Navajo rugs**. In the late 1800s, when weavers first introduced these sacred images for non-ceremonial use, controversy flared in the Navajo community. By the late 20th century, however, the appearance of Yei and Yei'bi'cheii in rug designs, and even in community murals and statues, became widely accepted and celebrated.

Yucca plants at White Sands National Monument near Alamogordo, NM

YUCCA

YUCK-ah Yucca plants, native to North and Central America and the Caribbean, are tough desert dwellers. With their slender, sword-like leaves displayed as an exploding, symmetrical bundle of sharp spikes, yuccas are an unmistakable symbol of the state—a status made official for the yucca's off-white flower in 1927.

Indeed, yuccas are not all prickle. A member of the lily family, this iconic plant produces a towering stalk covered with waxy, cream-colored flowers in spring. The beauty of these blooms inspired the Spanish to call them *Lamparas de Dios* or "Lamps of the Lord." Native inhabitants of the state found yucca to be a viable food source (the stem, fruits, and flowers are all edible), but even more importantly, recognized its roots, stem, and leaves to be remarkably versatile for other purposes. Not only could its roots be crushed and made into soap, its durable, fibrous leaves could easily be woven into rope and twine, sandals, and baskets, or made into fine paintbrushes (tools that many **Pueblo** potters still use today). *See also Pueblo Pottery.*

Vintage license plates hang on an old garage door in Cuba, NM

ZIA SYMBOL

The *zia*, featured on the New Mexico state flag and license plate, is an ancient symbol of the Rio Grande valley's Zia **Pueblo**. Representing the sun, the symbol's distinctive circular design with four rays radiating from each of its four sides encompasses the spiritual beliefs and life philosophies of the Zia people.

Each group of rays signifies the four cardinal directions of the earth, the four seasons of the year, the four periods of the day (morning, noon, evening, and night), and the four periods of life (childhood, youth, manhood, and old age). This ideology extends to man's four sacred obligations: a strong body, a clear mind, a pure spirit, and devotion to the welfare of his people. The circle, representative of life, binds these sacred divisions, without a beginning or end.

Although not protected by copyright, a state legislative act limits the specific dimensions of the Zia symbol for official use, as well as its colors—the royal red and yellow of Old Spain—thus protecting it from additional or inappropriate use beyond the Zia themselves.

Will Schuster's 2008 Zozobra in Santa Fe, NM • Courtesy of The Downtown Santa Fe Kiwanis Foundaion and Ray A. Valdez

ZOZOBRA

As staged during the autumnal Fiestas de Santa Fe, the wild 50-foot-tall marionette of Zozobra, or Old Man Gloom, is set afire to the roaring cheers of the crowd. Prior to his spectacular incineration, Zozobra looms over his observers and laments his fate with flapping arms and spinning eyes. Made of muslin, wood, and paint, he is reportedly stuffed with shredded divorce papers and police reports; it is hoped that their burning will help all involved to find relief.

The Fiesta has evolved greatly since it began in Santa Fe in 1712. First started to commemorate Don Diego de Vargas's (1643–1704) reconquest of the New Mexico territory in 1692 following the Pueblo Revolt of 1680, it has since become an annual local ritual that touches on that history, but also includes hugely popular events like the Zozobra kick-off and a children's pet parade.

Old Man Gloom, the modern Fiesta's centerpiece, officially came on board in 1926, two years after local artist Will Schuster (1893–1969) first created the spectacle for friends. Today, the Kiwanis Club of Santa Fe hosts the event.

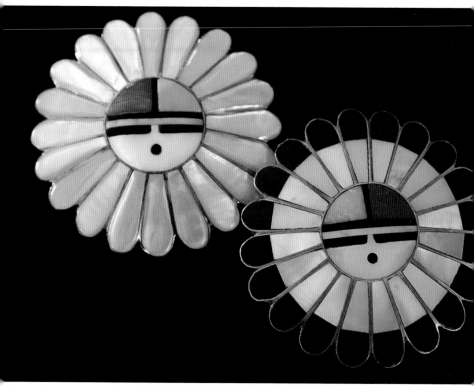

Sunface broaches made of jet, coral, turquoise, and mother-of-pearl (artists unknown)

ZUNI SUNFACE

This characteristic design of Zuni **Pueblo**, in northwestern New Mexico, represents a beneficent being said to bring good luck and ensure a bright future. As the spirit of the sun, the sunface characterizes one of the most important and powerful spirits, or *kokos* (similar to **kachinas**), in the Zuni pantheon.

The sunface design is most often crafted in **silver jewelry** using red coral, **turquoise**, jet, and mother-of-pearl. These materials represent the sacred colors of Mother Earth (red), Father Sky (blue), and the force of balance in the universe (black and white). Zuni artisans are well known for using these and other semi-precious stones in a fine jewelry-making technique called *inlay*. In this process, stones are sized and nestled together to create an even, colorful surface. Sometimes thin strips of silver are inserted between the stones; this delicate variation is known as *channel inlay. See also Silver Jewelry.*

NEW MEXICO'S HISTORY OF MIGRATION

• 800–1300s •

ANCESTRAL PUEBLOANS, the ancestors of the modern-day Pueblo people, enjoy the "Golden Age" of their culture.

• 1400s •

The historically nomadic **DINÉ** (Navajo) and **APACHE** tribes arrive in New Mexico and clash at times with the more sedentary **PUEBLOANS**. **COMMANCHE** and **UTE** Indians later establish themselves in the area.

• 1500s •

On a search for gold, Spanish **CONQUISTADORS** travel up El Camino Real (The King's Road) and discover Pueblos along the Rio Grande.

• 1600s •

Spanish **MISSIONARIES** descend upon Pueblos with the hopes to convert whole communities to Catholicism. In a coordinated effort, **PUEBLOANS** revolt in 1680 and expel the colonists, only to have them return in 1692 and resettle in surrounding communities.

• 1700s •

In an effort to further colonize the region, Spanish leaders award vast land grants to **HISPANIC SETTLERS**.

• 1800s •

Mexico gains independence from Spain in 1821, about the same time the first Anglo **TRADERS** arrive off the Santa Fe Trail. They soon begin to formalize a system of barter and trade on the frontier.

• 1800s, Cont. •

New Mexico becomes an official territory of the United States in 1850 as a result of the Mexican-American War.

The arrival of the railroad in 1878 encourages the development of ranching, mining, and railroad towns. These industries bring an influx of **RAILWORKERS, COWBOYS, MINERS, MERCHANTS, HOMESTEADERS,** and **TOURISTS** to the region, who introduce Anglo culture and help to transform the territory into the fabled Wild West.

ARTISTS and **WRITERS** become enchanted with the breathtaking landscape, rustic lifestyle, and exceptional light of the desert. Many take up residence and form influential artist societies, which thrive for decades.

• 1900s •

New Mexico becomes the 47th state in 1912. **TOURISTS,** who seek exotic experiences and "Indian curios," rediscover the region.

In 1943 the top-secret Manhattan Project brings **SCIENTISTS** to the isolated outpost of Los Alamos to build the world's first atomic bomb.

HIPPIES arrive in New Mexico in the 1960s. They are met with reticent tolerance from locals, who take up a few of their ideas.

• 2000s •

After an early history with Hollywood westerns, "Tamalewood" once again attracts **FILMMAKERS** to shoot mainstream and indie movies in the state.

NOT TO BE MISSED

Restaurants (Casual New Mexican)
El Patio • Albuquerque
Sophia's Place • Albuquerque
Mary and Tito's Cafe • Albuquerque
Owl Cafe • Albuquerque & San Antonio
Flying Star Cafe • Albuquerque & Bernalillo
The Frontier • Albuquerque
La Fonda Restaurant and Hotel • Santa Fe
Cafe Pasqual's • Santa Fe
Tomasitas • Santa Fe
Tia Sophia's • Santa Fe
The Shed • Santa Fe
The Plaza Cafe • Santa Fe
Bobcat Bite • Santa Fe
El Parasol • SF, Española & Los Alamos
Orlando's • Taos
Michael's Kitchen • Taos
El Bruno's • Cuba
Jerry's Cafe • Gallup
Mine Shaft Tavern • Madrid
Estella's Cafe • Las Vegas
Rancho de Chimayó • Chimayó
Chope's Bar & Cafe • La Mesa
Nellie's Cafe • Las Cruces

Attractions
International Balloon Fiesta • Albuquerque
Indian and Spanish Markets • Santa Fe
Santa Fe Opera • Santa Fe
Canyon Road • Santa Fe
Ten Thousand Waves Spa • Santa Fe
Palace of the Governors • Santa Fe
El Rancho de las Golondrinas • Santa Fe
High & Low Roads to Taos • Santa Fe-Taos
Tesuque Pueblo Flea Mkt • Tesuque
Shidoni (Sculpture Garden) • Tesuque
Mabel Dodge Luhan House • Taos
Taos Pueblo • Taos
Pecos National Historic Park • Pecos
Bosque del Apache • Socorro
El Santuario de Chimayó • Chimayó
White Sands Nat'l Monument • Alamogordo
Carlsbad Caverns Nat'l Park • Carlsbad
Chaco Culture Nat'l Hist Park • Nageezi
Bandelier National Monument • Los Alamos
Gila Cliff Dwellings Nat'l Mnmt • Silver City
Crownpoint Rug Auctions • Crownpoint
The Lightning Field • Quemado
Valles Caldera • Jemez Springs
Acoma Pueblo • Acoma Pueblo
Pueblo Feast Days and Dances • Statewide

Museums
Indian Pueblo Cultural Cntr • Albuquerque
The Albuquerque Museum • Albuquerque
Nat'l Hispanic Cultural Cntr • Albuquerque
Nat'l Mus of Nuclear Science & Hist • ABQ
Georgia O'Keeffe Museum • Santa Fe
Museum of International Folk Art • Santa Fe
Wheelwright Museum • Santa Fe
Museum of Spanish Colonial Art • Santa Fe
Museum of Indian Arts & Culture • Santa Fe
New Mexico Museum of Art • Santa Fe
Taos Art Museum & Fechin House • Taos
Harwood Museum of UNM • Taos
Millicent Rogers Museum • Taos
International UFO Museum • Roswell
Western NM University Museum • Silver City
NM Farm & Ranch Museum • Las Cruces
Deming Luna Mimbres Museum • Deming

ACKNOWLEDGEMENTS

To Jordan Parhad, Anne and Stan Friedlander, Martin Sobolewski, Bob, Carol, and Susanne Duffner, Javier Read de Alaniz, Virginia Alaniz, Fred Parhad, Drew Smith, Kristen St. John, Jon Weinberg, Amy Duchêne, Lynne Arany, Holly Anlian and family, Kelly Toscano, Laura Ryan, Diako Diakoff, Susan Littenberg-Hagler, Michael Hagler, Kevin O'Connell, Jesse Wine, Kimberly Gillem, Matt Gulley, Catherine Davila, Bronwyn Fox-Bern, William Quinby, Dennis Trujillo, Vince Valenzuela, and my parents, John and Carole Sobolewski—Thank You. Without your assistance, support, inspiration, and encouragement, this book would not have been possible.

CONTRIBUTORS

Nancy Harbert

Lynne Arany
CONSULTING EDITOR
www.inkprojects.com

Asia Pacific Offset
PRINTER
www.asiapacificoffset.com

Susanne Duffner
DESIGNER &
PHOTOGRAPHER
www.picapress.com

Alex Cashman
PHOTOGRAPHER

Phillip A. Russell
PHOTOGRAPHER

Jordan Parhad
PHOTOGRAPHER

Bob Snead
PHOTOGRAPHER
www.bobsnead.com

Louis C. Vest
PHOTOGRAPHER
OneEighteen Photography

Renée Ann Wirick
PHOTOGRAPHER
Renée's photographs can
be found on Flickr.com

ABOUT THE AUTHOR

Elisa Parhad
AUTHOR & PHOTOGRAPHER
www.elisaparhad.com

A cultural anthropologist at heart and by trade, Elisa Parhad is passionate about exploring place, space, design, and culture. She was first introduced to New Mexico as a child, when her family moved to Albuquerque from Seattle, Washington. After completing Bachelors degrees in Cultural Anthropology and International Business at the University of Texas at Austin, she spent eight years studying American subcultures and communities to inform marketing messaging and advertising campaigns. She lives in Los Angeles, California with her husband and son.

To submit comments, suggestions, photographs,
or to just say hello, please write to
hello@eyemusebooks.com.

To order this and other Guides for the Eyes visit www.eyemusebooks.com.